# ENDING THE WAR ON DRUGS

# ENDING THE WAR ON DRUGS

A Solution for America

BY DIRK CHASE ELDREDGE

Bridge Works Publishing Company
Bridgehampton, New York

First North American Edition

*Library of Congress Cataloging-in-Publication Data*

Eldredge, Dirk Chase, 1932–
Ending the war on drugs : a solution for America / Dirk Chase
Eldredge. — 1st ed.
p.    cm.
Includes bibliographical references and index.
ISBN 1-882593-24-3 (hardcover : alk. paper)
1. Narcotics, Control of—United States.   2. Drug traffic—United
States.   3. Drug legalization—United States.   I. Title.
HV5825.E468   1998
363.4'5'0973—dc21          98-14939

Published in the United States by Bridge Works Publishing Company,
Bridgehampton, New York

Distributed by National Book Network, Lanham, Maryland

2   4   6   8   10   9   7   5   3   1

Printed in the United States of America

# DEDICATION

———◦◦◦———

This book is about the future of our nation, about how we can deal with our difficult and complex drug problems in more constructive ways. Because it takes time to achieve change in a democracy, it is appropriate that this book be dedicated to those people in my life to whom the future belongs — my children and theirs. And so I dedicate it to my daughter Kim Gibler, her husband Scott and their children, Brittany, Taylor and Weston, as well as to my son Dirk, his wife Tamiko and their children, Chelsea, Chase, and Christina.

It is my hope that the facts, opinions and ideas presented herein will help make their world better.

# CONTENTS

# ACKNOWLEDGMENTS

———◦◦◦———

The inspiration for this book was provided by the courage and conviction of Judge James P. Gray of the Orange County, California, Superior Court, who openly and forcefully declared the war on drugs to be the public policy disaster it is, even though by doing so, he put his judicial career at risk. America needs more leaders and public servants of his character. He also provided valuable editorial advice during the book's formulation.

I am also deeply indebted to Gaylord E. (Nick) Nichols and Donne Moen for the many hours they spent reading and critiquing the original drafts. While not always agreeing with my opinions, they provided suggestions, criticism and encouragement.

My dear friend Thomas H. (Tom) Taylor, avoiding the role of critic, contributed many hours by reading and commenting positively on the original drafts. His insights and interest in the project have been immensely appreciated and valuable.

It has been my good fortune to work with Warren and Barbara Phillips, co-publishers of Bridge Works Publishing. They have become mentors and friends.

Finally, I must acknowledge the enormous support and encouragement on the part of my entire family and particularly my wife, Donna. Her radiant smile and nearly limitless patience with my preoccupation made the work both possible and pleasant.

# AUTHOR'S PREFACE

America's war on drugs is reminiscent of the Russian princess who sat weeping profusely at the death of the hero in a performance at the opera while, at the curb, her waiting carriage driver froze to death in a Moscow ice storm. America's policy makers are deeply preoccupied with waging the war on drugs. As they pursue that effort, the destructive, albeit unintended, consequences continue to pile up like the icy snows of Moscow.

Prohibition is the linchpin of our nation's drug policy. Prohibition has spawned, as it always does, a robust black market, which inevitably spins off many social pathologies and is a policy that can only fail because its objective — a drug-free America — is unrealistic and unattainable. When balanced on the societal scale, the dubious premise of somewhat fewer drug users under our present prohibitionist policies is far outweighed by the societal damage these policies cause.

The United States has 5 percent of the world's population but consumes 60 percent of its illicit drugs. The money generated to satisfy U.S. demand, at economically unsupportable black-market prices, is the root cause of drug-related corruption of public servants both at home and throughout our hemisphere. Our hard-won progress in race relations is threatened by the perception of many African Americans that the drug war is a racist plot. Our police, courts and prisons are inundated by a flood of drug cases. Our civil liberties are being eroded. The AIDS epidemic is worsened as our drug-war zeal causes us to continue, in most places, to forbid the availability of clean needles to injection-drug users. Grossly inflated black-market prices for drugs result in easy recruitment into the drug subculture of uninformed adolescents. Crime and violence accompany the illegal drug trade to the detriment of the guilty and the innocent alike. Like the Russian princess, the United States is so preoccupied with the present show that it is oblivious to what is going on in the real world.

This book will focus on the crime, corruption, and other unintended consequences of our quixotic war on drugs. It will show the folly of our present approach and the need for a new direction: legal, controlled distribution of drugs, which will replace prohibition with harm reduction not only for the user but for the nation at large.

I should state right up front that I am not an aging hippie or a liberal academic. I am a white, conservative Republican who has passed the Medicare milestone after a quarter century as a successful independent businessman. I have been married to the same woman for over forty years and have six grandchildren. My father was an alcoholic whose life was a disaster for himself and his family, because he was a true addict, one of many beset with personal problems with which they cannot successfully cope, a man who unsuccessfully tried to assuage his demons with the mood-changing drug alcohol. My father lived through Prohibition, and it did no more to prevent his self-destructive behavior than drug prohibition has done for today's seekers of excessive mind and mood alteration.

Because of my firsthand acquaintance with addiction, nothing in this book should be construed as being supportive of drug use. Excessive drug use, like excessive drinking and smoking, is dangerous to the health of the user and the citizenry at large. True addicts like my father have a problem that requires treatment by medical and/or mental health professionals. However, the drug war makes criminals of millions of otherwise solid, productive citizens who choose to use illegal drugs in the same way some use alcohol. These people are not like my father; they live productive lives and harm no one. The "try and die" concept promoted by the drug warriors does not square with the facts. Our perception of all drug users as addicts has been created by our propensity to focus on the sensational, often macabre aspects of these unfortunates, while tarring all drug users with the same brush.

My solution for America offers help to all: first, the creation of a state government–sponsored and –enforced policy of distribution and sale of drugs; thus re-directing the profits from the pockets of the cartels into state governments, where, by law, they would be used to combat drug use and abuse. The crime and violence currently accompanying illegal drug use and sales would cease. With more funds for professional treatment of the addicted, and most of all, a unified American effort to expand drug education and research, our country could concentrate on prevention instead of prohibition. I am not the first, nor will I be the last, to point out the counterproductiveness of America's present drug policies, but the truth and logic of my position encourage me that my proposal will eventually prevail.

Dirk Chase Eldredge
Long Beach, California
July 1, 1998

# ENDING THE WAR ON DRUGS

# 1

---

# DRUG USERS AND DRUGS:
# MYTHS VERSUS FACTS

## Needed: More Light, Less Heat

Few subjects exist in America today about which more misinformation circulates than the myths surrounding illicit drugs and their
users. Tens of millions of people in America either have used or are
using illegal drugs for none other than recreational purposes. They
use them in moderation, mostly in private, and their lives do not
become subordinate to the substance, be it cocaine, marijuana, or
sometimes even heroin. As with alcohol, some start their use in a
controlled mode and later cross the line into dependence or addiction,
but abusers are a small minority of illegal-drug consumers. A study of
cocaine-use patterns illustrates this with its finding that less than 1
percent of those who had ever tried cocaine became daily users.[1]

Robert Reno, writing in the December 16, 1993 issue of *The
Miami Herald*, did an engaging job of putting drug abuse into
perspective:

> *Think of it: Seven percent of Americans have heart conditions.
> Eleven percent have high blood pressure, and 12 percent have
> arthritis. Five percent have hemorrhoids, and 3 percent have
> varicose veins. The figure for smokers is 27 percent and for
> users of alcohol, 51 percent. But only 0.9 percent regularly use
> cocaine, according to the National Institute on Drug Abuse.
> Even if this figure is understated, you have to more than
> double it to equal the national rate for ingrown toenails or*

*chronic constipation, which are 2.3 percent and 1.9 percent,
respectively. Drug-related violence may seem epidemic, but
clearly, drug abuse isn't when compared with most diseases.*[2]

In fact, Mr. Reno's satiric analysis greatly overstates the percentage of the population that uses cocaine daily. The NIDA study actually said that 0.9 percent of those who had ever used cocaine became daily users. Because those who have ever used cocaine are a fraction of the population, less than 1 percent of that fraction would be a great deal less than .9 percent of the entire population. The actual percentage of the population that uses cocaine on a daily basis is closer to .002 percent. While that is a serious problem for those involved, it is hardly an epidemic.

Some who use drugs are deserving of the disdain heaped on them by the nonusing public, because they have allowed drugs to control and consume their lives. They are individuals for whom drugs have become the focus of their existence. These are the people who are the drug users' equivalent of the alcohol users' alcoholic — in short, users who are drug-dependent or addicted. This breed is the daily fare of the media, and the public perception grows that all drug users fall into this devastated category.

## Demonizing All Drug Use Helps No One

David Lewis, M.D., director of the Brown University Center for Alcohol and Addiction Studies, helped develop a 1995 study on cocaine use for the World Health Organization (WHO). The results of the study, as reported by Dr. Lewis to Robert Curley, national editor of *Alcoholism & Drug Abuse Weekly*, are quite at odds with the popular perception of cocaine and cocaine users, and will shock those attuned to contemporary drug-war rhetoric. Curley's summation:

*There is no indication that cocaine is a drug that automatically
leads to loss of control. We have a very hard time with illegal*

*drugs because we tend to condemn any use at all. "Try and die"*
*is the message from U.S. drug policy. . . .*

*Occasional use of cocaine is the most common pattern,*
*and occasional users generally experience few problems related*
*to their use.*[3]

Policy makers tend to view drugs in black and white terms, but
as the WHO study illustrates, even use of cocaine is a grayer issue
than is commonly acknowledged. Curley predicts, "[Society] will get
fed up with using incarceration to treat addiction. There will be a
gradual shift to treatment and prevention, and less criminal justice
attention to drug possession and maybe drug sales."

There is much statistical evidence to support assertions about
occasional use being the rule rather than the exception. The following table, based on a 1991 nationwide household study of both
cocaine and marijuana use, shows that occasional users outnumber
those who use the drugs weekly or more often.[4]

### Types of Drug Users (as Percentage of All Users)

| Frequency of Use | Marijuana | Cocaine |
|---|---|---|
| Less than once a month | 52% | 74% |
| Once a month | 21% | 16% |
| Once a week or more often | 27% | 10% |
| Total users in past year | 100% | 100% |

## Why Use Illicit Drugs?

As with participation in any form of censured behavior, individual
motives are often complex. When subjected to close scrutiny, however, they are classifiable into one or more of the following:

*Peer Pressure.* This is at once the most frustrating and most
common reason, particularly among the rebellious young. The urge to
conform and be accepted, however unwise, is a powerful motivator.

Though it is most often discussed as a characteristic of teenagers, it is also a strong motivation in the twenties and, in some cases, even into the thirties. The vast majority of drug use is done by those from 15 to 35, and most users are introduced to drugs by a friend who is using, not by the popularly blamed "drug pusher." Sometimes this can be one and the same person. It should come as no surprise that it usually takes the reassurance of a trusted friend to inhale a foreign substance up one's nose for the first time.

*To Reduce Inhibitions.* Many users have been introduced, or reintroduced, to illicit drugs at a party or other informal social gathering. As the party begins to wane, someone suggests one form of drug or another to "get things going." Alcohol is the most popular social lubricant, but illegal drugs run a contentious second. Instant bonding can often result from the passing of a joint back and forth in a social setting. The lowered inhibitions resulting from the marijuana can turn the painfully shy into the life of the party. To some, this is a powerful attraction.

*To Experience Altered Consciousness.* The lure of this experience is as old as life itself. Animals are known to seek grazing material that can inebriate. Since the dawn of time, humans have enjoyed the juice of fermented fruits and grains in their various forms. Children seek to alter their conscious experience by twirling about until they drop from dizziness. Many people seek alteration in the hope that it will enhance their creativity or productivity. This has worked wonders for some, tragedy for others. The greatest danger to those who seek to use drugs in this way is the pharmacological fact that the longer one uses drugs, the more is required to achieve the sought-after high. Some people with serious psychological problems seek to escape their dark, personal prisons through the medium of drugs. Others who are temporarily down simply want to feel better. Aldous Huxley, the British philosopher and author who, during the 1950s, experimented extensively with mescaline, an hallucinogenic, said this about the demand for drugs: "Most men and women lead lives at the worst so painful, at the best so monotonous, poor, and limited that the urge to escape, the longing to transcend themselves, if only for a few moments, is and always has been one of the principal appetites of the soul."

*To Explore Oneself.* This pursuit can take many forms; experimentation with drugs is among the most popular and was almost the mantra of the 1960s. Those who would use drugs for this reason will profit from the experience related in an 1870 lecture by Oliver Wendell Holmes, celebrated American physician and author:

> *I once inhaled a pretty full dose of ether, with the determination to put on record, at the earliest moment of regaining consciousness, the thought I should find uppermost in my mind. The mighty music of the triumphal march into nothingness reverberated through my brain, and filled me with a sense of infinite possibilities, which made me an archangel for a moment. The veil of eternity was lifted. The one great truth which underlies all human experience and is the key to all the mysteries that philosophy has sought in vain to solve, flashed upon me in a sudden revelation. Henceforth all was clear: a few words had lifted my intelligence to the level of the knowledge of the cherubim. As my natural condition returned, I remembered my resolution; and staggering to my desk, I wrote, in ill-shaped, straggling characters, the all-embracing truth still glimmering in my consciousness. The words were these (children may smile; the wise will ponder): "A strong smell of turpentine prevails throughout."*

A strong smell of self-delusion surrounds efforts at self-realization through drug use, yet the notion remains a powerful attraction.

## The Ordinary Majority

Illegal drug users come from a wide variety of circumstances. What is unique about drug users is the misconception that they are mostly drug-crazed, gun-toting thugs ready to rob or kill for their next fix. In fact, most illegal drug users are quite ordinary citizens. They have homes, mortgages, children in Little League. Most are gainfully employed.

Illustrative of this fact is a group of would-be drug buyers who were arrested in a police operation in Lowell, Massachusetts, in July, 1993. Citizens of Lowell, increasingly concerned about the numbers coming to their city to purchase illicit drugs, spurred the Lowell police force into action. In a one-day sweep it arrested nineteen buyers. Their profiles provide an interesting, if unscientific, look at who is using drugs. Along with seven unemployed buyers, the police arrested a student hairdresser, a fast-food cook, a computer salesman, a registered nurse, a firefighter, a truck driver, two roofers, a machine operator, a carpenter, a telephone lineman, and a dry-wall installer.[5]

Examples of the down-and-out drug user abound in the press and electronic media. Less familiar are the majority of users who live normal lives apart from their drug-related activities. To fully understand the drug problem and its many ramifications, it is imperative that we see the universe of users as it really is, not as we imagine it to be.

## High-Profile Users

Celebrity use of drugs works a dichotomy on the public's drug consciousness. On the one hand, the arrest of a celebrated entertainer or the suspension of a high-profile athlete provides a warning of the dangers of drug use. But it also serves to glamorize drug use to the impressionable young.

Arnold Washton, a Manhattan psychologist, reports that drug use among Wall Street executives is widespread.[6] Some firms have become concerned enough to implement employee drug testing and assistance programs for those whose drug use has deteriorated into abuse. A combination of high incomes and the desire to relieve the stress of pressure-laden jobs surely contribute to the prevalence of drugs in the financial nerve center of America.

## Impaired Users

A 29-year-old resident of south-central Los Angeles who contracted multiple sclerosis ten years ago provides a poignant insight into the world of the handicapped drug user:

> *If I were in a different area, I wouldn't be doing what I do now. I smoke marijuana and crack cocaine. I don't rob. I don't steal. I hustle, I wash cars and cut grass.*
>
> *My average day is like this: I wake up and thank the Lord. I eat my breakfast, go out, get my little weed and smoke my little weed and get me some beer. The crack ain't an everyday thing.*[7]

Physical impairment is not the only handicap common among those involved with drugs. Both adult and juvenile drug abusers (as distinct from users) are frequently known to have serious psychological disorders that preceded their involvement with drugs. In a 1994 study of 54 patients in a drug treatment center for college students, 37 percent were found to have suffered from psychiatric problems prior to their drug use. The most common psychiatric illnesses were depression, phobias, panic disorder and obsessive-compulsive disorder.[8]

Illicit drugs are not alone in their appeal to the emotionally troubled. Nicotine, the highly addictive legal drug found in tobacco, is the object of a spirited battle being waged by the inmates of mental hospitals around the country. Caught up in the anti-smoking wave engulfing the nation, smoking has been banned in many hospitals. Some of these institutions are mental hospitals whose patients are fighting hard to maintain their right to smoke, in spite of the acknowledged health hazards. It happens that while 30 percent of the adult population smoke, 88 percent of schizophrenics do, as do 70 percent of those suffering from mania.[9] These patients argue convincingly that they are deserving of special consideration, as their pleasures and diversions are few enough.

## Heavy Users

Most drug studies classify those who use weekly, or more often, as heavy users. A significant study of 228 heavy cocaine users was conducted between 1985 and 1987 by a research team of three drug experts headed by Dan Waldorf, Research Sociologist and Project Director at the Institute for Scientific Analysis, Craig Reinarman, Associate Professor of Sociology at the University of California at Santa Cruz, a prolific author on the subject of illegal drugs, and Sheigla Murphy, co-principal investigator of a National Institute on Drug Abuse study of women and cocaine. Their solid body of research, published by Temple University Press, provides us with insight on the world of the heavy drug user. To be included in the study, the 228 subjects had to be using two or more grams of cocaine a week (about $200 worth at the time) for at least six months, or have used at least some cocaine every day for a minimum of one year. These minimums, which were exceeded by most participants, placed their use in the heaviest-using 5 percent of the 24,000,000 Americans who had ever used cocaine.[10] The term "heavy cocaine user," then, is a well-deserved designation for this study's respondents. The most significant finding of the study was that the best predictor of the result of cocaine use was the investment the user had in his or her own conventional life. The investment could be in the form of either family or career. Lacking either of these anchors to windward, the odds of cocaine use becoming abuse soared. The authors concluded:

> . . . *however powerful a drug may be, its effects are always mediated by the norms, practices, and circumstances of its users. Such a finding does not lend itself to simplistic slogans about the dangers of drugs. Nor will it lead to simple solutions to our drug problems. But if it forces us to think in more complicated ways about drug use and its cultural context, then we will be in a better position to develop rational public policies toward drug problems.*[11]

One of the more surprising profiles that emerged from the study was Patty (not her real name). This heavy user was a professional economist, a mother, a Girl Scout leader, and a part-time dealer. Her long-term use of cocaine was incidental to her life, not its focus.

Another subject from the study ultimately became an attorney. He had started using drugs in high school, continued while attending a major university, participated regularly in athletics, and worked steadily at a variety of typical student jobs. He quit using for several reasons. Fear that a felony conviction would preclude his becoming a lawyer, severe sinus problems due to his cocaine snorting, and pressure from his family all contributed to his decision. Quitting abruptly, he experienced no serious withdrawal symptoms, and did not use at all for two years. He reported that he now uses cocaine only occasionally.[12]

While the percentage of heavy users of cocaine is not large, the numbers are growing, even as the total number of users diminishes. There were over 3 million fewer cocaine users in 1995 than in 1988, yet the number of heavy users grew by 10 percent between 1991 and 1995 alone.[13] This growth has not escaped the notice of policy makers. Lee P. Brown, when he was director of the White House Office of Drug Control Policy, stated that administration drug strategy would shift resources into treatment in an effort to address the fact that there were 1.1 million drug users who could benefit from treatment for whom no facilities existed.[14] Where the funds would come from was not specified.

Administration estimates are that 20 percent of cocaine users consume 66 percent of the nation's cocaine,[15] whereas a hard-drinking 13 percent of us who drink alcohol consume 66 percent of that drug.[16]

## Drug Deaths in Perspective

While illicit drugs have a well-deserved reputation as agents of death, contrary to the perception of the public, many more deaths result from trafficking in drugs than from actual drug use.

Studies find that 80 percent of the deaths associated with heroin and cocaine are the result, not of drug use, but of the illegal nature of the market.[17] An analysis of crack cocaine–related homicides in New York City found that 85 percent were "systemic," that is, they were related to the dangers of the black-market distribution system rather than to any economic or pharmacologic compulsivity on the part of a user.[18]

When compared to the annual number of premature deaths from tobacco (400,000) and from alcohol (100,000), drug deaths lag far behind. It would be difficult to support a figure of more than 30,000 deaths from illegal drug use, even if the assumption were made that half of all homicides are drug-related.[19] These individual tragedies must be viewed in the context of the 77,000,000 Americans, 37 percent of the population over 11 years of age (as of 1993), who have consumed illegal drugs — some once, some occasionally, some habitually.[20]

## How Inevitable Is Abuse?

To some, the term "controlled use of narcotics" is as much an oxymoron as "military intelligence," or "government efficiency." We have been conditioned to believe it defines the impossible. The fact is that controlled use of narcotics is not only possible but predominant. Furthermore, as a nation we will never be able to approach the drug problem intelligently and effectively until we recognize this and other seemingly unpalatable truths about illicit drugs. On the subject of controlled or occasional use of cocaine, Waldorf, Reinarman, and Murphy reported:

> *To judge from the NIDA surveys of the incidence of cocaine use, the majority of users in the United States . . . use the drug occasionally, but do not abuse it. They experience pleasant effects and avoid unpleasant effects. Above all, they are very moderate in their use patterns. They do not lose control, go on*

*heavy binges, use it every day, or experience cocaine-related problems.*

*We were surprised to learn that many people who had previously used cocaine heavily could return to occasional or ceremonial use and not lose control. Indeed, more than half (52.6 percent) of the seventy-six untreated quitters we interviewed had done just that.*[21]

The notion that using drugs, particularly the major drugs such as cocaine and heroin, will inevitably result in dependence or addiction, has been promoted either overtly or by implication in antidrug polemics. Well intentioned as they are, these baseless claims are soon discovered, either from users' personal experience or from peers, to be untrue. Such myths seriously impede the cause of effective drug prevention education. Just as we cannot arrest our way out of the drug problem, neither can we frighten our way out. It bears repeating: Fewer than 1 percent of those who try cocaine become daily users.

Factors that come into play in determining a person's susceptibility to moving from experimentation to addiction or dependence include the mind-set of the user: What is he looking for from the drug? How stable is she? Does she have a predisposition to compulsive behavior? How is the drug ingested? What is the setting of the use? Are the users alone or in a social setting when using? What drug and how much is being ingested? How much has the drug been diluted? How frequent is the use? The difference between abstinence, occasional use, and addiction or dependence is a matter of personal choice. Drugs don't overpower people. People succumb to drugs.

## Addiction and Dependence

An attempt to understand true addiction and the difference between it and its close relative, dependence, will reward any serious student of drug use. The two terms are often confused because they are used almost interchangeably due to the ambiguity of and consequent disagreement about the term "addiction."

True addiction is much more difficult to cure than dependence. Addiction has an important physiological component, while dependence is largely psychological, with some physical components. For a substance to be truly addictive in the medical sense, it must encompass three characteristics: *reinforcement, tolerance,* and *withdrawal.* A substance with only one or two of these characteristics is not addictive.

Cigarette smoking is the most common true addiction.[22] A so-called "addiction" to chocolate may be the most common dependence. Both substances bring pleasure to the user, at least in the short run, so they share the first important characteristic of addiction, *reinforcement.* Simply stated, reinforcement is the pleasure-giving quality of a substance that will cause the user to repeat the experience. With cigarettes it is the nicotine-caused, amiable euphoria the smoker enjoys; with chocolate, it is the love of the flavor and the mild lift from the combination of caffeine, and caffeine-like theobromine.

*Tolerance* is the second characteristic of addiction. A truly addictive substance must cause the user to develop a tolerance that results in an escalation of the amount of the substance required to achieve the sought-after result during the first five or so years of use. The common progression of the cigarette smoker who starts with a few smokes a day and builds up to one or more packs a day is a good example. On the other hand, even people who consider themselves "addicted" to chocolate are not known to require increasing amounts of chocolate over the years to satisfy their cravings — so chocolate lacks the second characteristic of a true addictive substance.

*Withdrawal,* the third characteristic that must be present in a truly addictive substance, is composed of any group of physical symptoms that occurs when a regularly taken drug is discontinued, and disappears when the drug is resumed. Upon medical advice or a critical look at the waistline, one can usually stop consuming large amounts of chocolate. Most would miss it for a time, but the craving usually passes in a matter of weeks. Not so with a cigarette smoker who has become addicted to nicotine. The physical (as well as emotional) turmoil of throwing off an addiction to nicotine is a horror because the body has developed a physiological need. The same withdrawal symptoms are true of alcohol.

When a drug user must ingest a substance to satisfy a physical need, consumption of that substance becomes a compulsive, defensive act to avoid withdrawal. The excessive consumption of cocaine is therefore classified as a habit, or dependence, rather than a true addiction, because upon cessation of use, physical withdrawal symptoms do not occur.

Repeated drug use and the accompanying tolerance are more likely to develop into abuse when the user's objective is to counter the effects of life's problems — familial, social or economic — and also because some drugs, cocaine being the best example, can enhance performance in the short run. A stimulant, cocaine has increased productivity within a spectrum of users, from waitresses to novelists. But when the element of tolerance kicks in, suddenly the user finds that she needs ever-increasing amounts to achieve the high she has come to enjoy. Body and budget suffer from what was initially a positive experience. But cessation of cocaine use, no matter how profoundly challenging, doesn't qualify as withdrawal.

By contrast, heroin withdrawal causes not only psychological distress but intense physical discomfort marked by tremors and severe, flu-like symptoms, which can persist for many days. Of the three major illicit drugs, heroin is the only one carrying with it the appalling physical discomfort of withdrawal.

Neither psychological nor physical dependence is easy to cure, but psychological dependence is less difficult. Generally, a physically dependent user is in all likelihood psychologically dependent as well.

The in-depth study of heavy cocaine users by Waldorf, Reinarman, and Murphy contains dozens of examples of subjects who used substantially for years and quit without any severe physiological symptoms. Here is the assessment:

> *. . . the vast majority of our quitters reported, at most, minor withdrawal symptoms after quitting. Some reported cravings for cocaine, but these were more often seen as fleeting, transitory, and manageable. Very few reported anything like the severe physiological symptoms reported by alcoholics and opiate addicts.*[23]

Some scientific observers have known for years that much of the histrionics of supposed cocaine "withdrawal" actually are learned behavior on the part of the user.[24] He has read and heard what withdrawal is supposed to be like, and so he behaves that way. While this makes the suffering no less genuine, there is no physiological basis for a withdrawal reaction.

Most cocaine abusers "mature out" of their habit in five years or so. Heroin abuse, on the other hand, frequently continues for decades. Also, on average, heroin attracts a more reckless drug abuser than cocaine, because until recently it was almost always injected.

## Differences Between Drugs

The table below compares a variety of drugs with the three characteristics of addiction. Zero means the characteristic has no significance in that drug; 1 the characteristic is present but not important; 2 the means characteristic is significant; and 3 the means characteristic is strongly significant.[25]

## Comparison of Drugs' Characteristics

| Drug | Reinforcement | Tolerance | Withdrawal |
|------|---------------|-----------|------------|
| Alcohol | 2 | 1 | 3 |
| Barbiturates | 2 | 3 | 3 |
| Cocaine | 3 | 2 | 1 |
| Hallucinogens | 1 | 0 | 0 |
| Heroin | 2 | 3 | 3 |
| Marijuana | 2 | 1 | 1 |
| Nicotine | 2 | 2 | 2 |

## Addiction and Dependence Both Harm Society

From a societal perspective, differentiating between addiction and dependence confers a dubious distinction. In each case, the individual is dysfunctional, a problem to himself and his family. Mere possession constitutes criminal behavior. Consequently, the habitual crack user and the heroin addict pose a similar problem to society.

## Drug Use Is No Longer Declining

Until recently, the number of drug users had declined steadily since the peak years of the late 1970s. That slide came to an abrupt end in 1992. The Substance Abuse and Mental Health Services Administration's household survey, based on face-to-face interviews with over 17,700 people age 12 and older, taken yearly since 1979, showed a minor increase in the number of users between 1992 and 1993. By itself, the increase was not statistically significant, but it was important because it was the first increase since 1979 and thus reversed a 14-year decline. This study defined a user as a person who had ingested an illicit drug one or more times in the prior month. Between 1979 and 1992, the number of users declined from 25.4 million to 12.0 million but in 1993 the number increased to 12.3

million. This upward trend has persisted since then: The latest figures released for 1996 showed 13 million regular users, a 7 percent increase in three years.[26]

## Young People Are Setting the Trend

Even more troublesome is that drug use among our school-age population is increasing. According to data from the twenty-third national survey conducted by the University of Michigan and released on December 18, 1997, illicit drug use among American schoolchildren rose again in 1997. The survey included approximately 51,000 students in 429 secondary schools. The increase in the proportion of students using any illicit drug in the 12 months prior to the survey continued the steady increase that began in 1992. The survey showed that use among twelfth-graders had risen from 27 to 40 percent during the period from 1992 to 1997.

Observing this evidence not only of increased use but also of an acceleration in that increase, one might reasonably ask if recent generations are beginning to lose the cognitive chromosome. Not so: What has occurred is a steep decline in the attention we as a society are paying to antidrug education and prevention. A recent study by the Center for Media and Public Affairs reports that in 1990, stories about illegal drugs constituted 28 percent of all crime news on the three major television channels (ABC, CBS, and NBC). By 1996 that was down to 7 percent.[27]

Anyone who doubts the efficacy of media coverage in warning about dangerous behavior should study what it has done to reduce cigarette consumption in America. Twenty million people quit smoking between 1965 and 1975. From 1975 to 1993, the number of packs of cigarettes smoked per year, per person, dropped from 206 to 127.[28] This astonishing, life-saving progress is largely due to the attention focused by the media and some state governments on the dangers of smoking. The claims were factual and demonstrable.

## Are They Bad Because They're Problematic Users, or Vice Versa?

Two important points deserve restatement here. First, a very small percentage of users develop into problematic users, and second, such usage can frequently be reversed. Yet problematic cocaine and heroin users increased by about 10 percent between 1991 and 1995, while the percentage of occasional users fell about 35 percent, according to figures released by the Office of National Drug Control Policy.[29]

Problematic users account for a large share of total drug consumption. As stated previously, 20 percent of cocaine users consume 66 percent of the cocaine in America. The typical heavy user will consume eight times more than the average recreational user, thus he accounts for the lion's share of demand.[30] To support their habit these users commit between one third and one half of the street crime in America.[31]

Data on 581 California men who were problematic users, gathered from a compulsory drug treatment program for criminal offenders in 1964 and followed up on again in 1975 and 1986, provide rare insight. The ethnic makeup of the group was as follows: 36 percent white, 56 percent Hispanic, and 8 percent African American. The average age was 25. More than 80 percent had been arrested before they were 18, and more than 60 percent had started using drugs before they were 20 years old. Not a scientifically representative group of drug users, nor even of heavy drug users, the study illustrates both the downside of drug use and that even the worst cases can sometimes be redeemed.[32]

## Summary of Drug Treatment Program Study

|  | 1964 (%) | 1975 (%) | 1986 (%) |
|---|---|---|---|
| Confirmed dead | 0 | 13 | 28 |
| Could not find | 0 | 11 | 11 |
| In prison | 100 | 18 | 12 |
| Still using, but not in prison | 0 | 29 | 24 |
| Clean or controlled, not in prison | 0 | 29 | 25 |
| Totals | 100 | 100 | 100 |

It is jarring that 22 years later, nearly two out of three were either dead, still in prison, or locked in their own personal prison of drug use.

Of the deaths, 29 percent were homicides, suicides, or accidents, 32 percent died of drug overdose, while the remaining 39 percent died from other causes, including tobacco and alcohol use. The average age at death was just over 40.

Significantly, long-term heavy users had a smaller chance for recovery. The percentage who were clean or controlled and not in prison actually declined in the 11 years from 1975 to 1986.

## A Glossary of Illicit Drugs

Cocaine is the product of the coca leaf, which has been chewed for centuries as a mild narcotic by the Andean Indians. About 90 percent of the coca leaf is imported from Peru and nearby Bolivia to be processed into cocaine paste and powder in the thousands of processing labs sequestered in the jungles and valleys of Colombia. The remainder of the coca leaf is home-grown in Colombia.[33]

The conversion of the raw coca leaf into cocaine requires so-called precursor chemicals, solvents such as kerosene, acids like sulfuric or hydrochloric, and highly volatile ether or acetone. Approximately nine chemicals are used in the entire process from leaf to paste to powder, and most have substitutes that will also work. Obtaining these chemicals in sufficient quantities and moving them to the remote, hidden labs where they are used is a lively smuggling industry in itself. For instance, it requires between 65 and 130 gallons of kerosene to produce a single kilogram (2.2 pounds) of cocaine. Benzene or even gasoline can be substituted, at peril.[34]

In 1988 the United States passed the Chemical Diversion and Trafficking Act in an effort to control trade in these chemicals and discourage the production of cocaine. Unfortunately, this act has only served to complicate the business of our legitimate chemical producers and distributors and cause the drug dealers to look to other countries for these widely available commodities. When the act was passed in 1988, a little over half of the chemicals imported by Colombia came from the United States. By 1990, only one sixth came from the United States.[35] Yet there had been no decline in cocaine production.

Often, kerosene is replaced by benzene, a highly toxic chemical known to cause leukemia even at very low doses. As a result, a dangerous drug, cocaine, can be made far more so by being laced with benzene. By the DEA's estimate, 4 million to 5 million Americans may be "systematically exposing themselves to benzene."[36] Like so much other drug war legislation, the Chemical Diversion and Trafficking Act has made a bad matter worse.

Powder cocaine, which has been around since the late 1800s, is usually snorted (inhaled) through the nose and absorbed into the blood stream through the mucous membrane of the nasal passage. Much less frequently, it is dissolved in water and injected, or sprinkled on tobacco or marijuana and smoked.

Crack cocaine is simply powder cocaine with baking soda and water added. This mixture hardens into a rocklike cake that is then broken into small pebbles and sold for as little as $5. Before crack's introduction in the early 1980s, the minimum buy of regular cocaine was $50 to $100; a cheap form of cocaine, crack was very attractive to the poor.

Crack is ingested by heating it until it emits vapors, which are inhaled. Because crack enters via the lungs, it reaches the bloodstream much more quickly and in more concentrated form, producing a much faster, more intense euphoria.

The practice of freebasing — or "basing," as it is sometimes called — came about due to the decline in the cost of cocaine as a result of increased supply. Cocaine has dropped in price from $50,000 per kilo in 1980 to $12,000–$20,000 per kilo today, depending on local market conditions. At the same time, purity soared from 30 percent pure cocaine hydrochloride to 80 percent.[37] Freebase is produced by heating cocaine with water, ammonia, and ether; crystalline flakes of cocaine are formed, free of the impurities and solids that resulted from the original production process. The flakes cannot be snorted, so they are heated in a pipe and the vapors inhaled. This method of ingestion, as with crack cocaine, produces a much faster, more powerful high than snorting, particularly true of the first experience. It is said that a major reason for the stronger habit-forming qualities of freebase is that users keep trying, albeit unsuccessfully, to recapture the euphoria of that first experience. Robin Williams once commented, "Why do they call it freebase? It's not free, you can lose your home on that stuff. They ought to call it home base!"

The process of producing freebase, with its reliance on highly flammable ether, is dangerous. When the concoction blew up in comedian Richard Pryor's face, he was severely burned. After that well-publicized event, the popularity of freebase waned, but it has by no means disappeared.

America's appetite for heroin is showing an alarming increase. Some drug warriors are comparing heroin's increasing popularity to the crack epidemic of the early 1980s. While that seems an overstatement, there is no denying the growth in both the demand and supply of this powerful narcotic. The popularity factor of a given drug is cyclical; like other fads, it waxes and wanes. Cocaine and its progeny, crack, were the drugs of choice throughout the 1980s.

Heroin has gained on them during the 1990s. Not surprisingly, price is an important factor in the relative popularity of drugs. By the mid-1990s the price per gram of pure heroin had dropped steeply, from about $1,655 in 1988 to an average of $984.[38] Another reason for heroin's growing use is its greatly increased purity. In the mid-1980s, 5 to 7 percent purity was the rule on the street. Today, heroin purity ranges from 56 to 76 percent, with some seized samples running above 90 percent.[39]

When heroin purity was expressed in single-digit percentages the only practical way to ingest the drug was by injection. At the higher degrees of purity, the drug can be snorted or smoked like cocaine. This does away with the needle and its attendant invasiveness, plus the ever-present danger of AIDS. The result is a drug that is, to borrow a term from the computer world, more user-friendly.

Both the lower price and increased purity of heroin can be traced in part to Colombia's aggressive drug dealers. In 1992 the Colombian government was shocked to learn from a police report that some 50,000 acres of opium poppies were under cultivation within its borders, amounting to 9 percent of the world's crop.[40] These beautiful flowers are the source of the gum that is processed to become opium and heroin.

Colombian poppies are mostly being grown in areas controlled by Marxist guerrillas. Heroin is a particularly appealing product because a kilo, even at its decreased price, sells for ten times as much as a kilo of cocaine.

A Marxist rebel or Colombian peasant farmer can earn $90,000 per acre for each planting of poppies. Having nothing to lose, too many poverty-stricken peasants are willing to roll the drug dice.

But there are good reasons why 23 times more Americans have tried marijuana and 8 times more have tried cocaine than have tried heroin.[41] Long considered the most self-destructive of drug users, for the most part, the heroin-abusing population is a lawless, irresponsible subset, to whom the legal status of drugs makes even less difference than it does to users in general. Education as a preventive, and treatment when that fails, are the *only* strategies that have a chance with these unfortunates. They are a microcosm of the drug problem: We can try to minimize the number of heroin addicts, but there is no hope of eliminating the genre.

There is also a dire downside to heroin's increased purity: death. In June 1993, in Florida, three close friends unknowingly bought some very strong heroin, and all three injected it. Two of them died at the scene. Mike Stillwell, who lives near Pompano Beach, was the lucky one who survived. After sneaking out of the hospital to attend the funeral of his best friend, he said, "This stuff will kill you. . . . The word's gotta get out. Don't do it. Please don't do it."[42] At about the same time, in Vancouver, British Columbia, unusually pure heroin was blamed for the deaths of five people in a single day. The day happened to be "Welfare Wednesday," the day when welfare checks were issued.[43] Nationwide emergency-room visits caused by heroin and its fellow opiate, morphine, rose 44 percent in the first half of 1993 over the same period in 1992.[44]

Heroin is not alone among illicit drugs in its uncertain quality. The total absence of quality control is a universal characteristic of the black market. The drug dealer can, and does, dilute his product with everything from baking soda to brick dust. He answers to no one but his own greed. There are no contracts, no legal means of enforcement, and no rules of law. If the user lives to complain about quality, he is either ignored or the matter is settled by violence.

The assurance of predictable doses of unquestioned quality and purity is one of the most important advantages of the controlled, legal distribution of drugs compared to the present underground market. As long as either buyers or sellers are considered by society to be criminals, there is no way to insure the quality or consistency of any product.

Marijuana or pot, weed, grass, hemp, Mary Jane — whatever one calls it — is by far the most widely used illicit drug in America. One of every three Americans 12 or older has tried it, including the President and Vice President of the United States. The number of people who have used pot is three times greater than users of cocaine, its closest competitor. Unlike cocaine use, which declined throughout the 1980s and into the 1990s, marijuana use, after a similar decline in the 1980s, began increasing in 1991.[45] That increase continued through the mid-1990s.

Prior to the 1960s, marijuana was smoked mostly by minorities and musicians. Much lore surrounded the substance. Some characterized it as a drug capable of investing users with superhuman strength and inciting them to murderous violence. The term "reefer madness" was born of this misinformation, and that pall hung over marijuana use until the 1960s, when its use spread via the era's flower children.

Marijuana is the product of the hemp plant, *Cannabis sativa*, which also produces the fiber used to make hemp rope and textiles. It has been a valuable commercial crop for hundreds of years. The plant's intoxicating chemical, Tetrahydrocannibinol (THC), is in the resin excreted by its flowering top, especially that of the female plant. The amount of resin determines the strength of the product and varies widely among the various strains. If the hemp plant is simply chopped up, mixing leaves, stalks and resin-rich tops, a low-potency marijuana results. If carefully cultivated female tops are gathered before seeds form, they are sticky with resin, highly aromatic, and very potent.[46] When the resin itself is collected and pressed into cakes, it is called hashish. The resin can be extracted with solvents in a process similar to turning coca leaves into cocaine. When the resin is concentrated in this manner, the resulting thick, oily liquid is called hash oil. All of these products can be either smoked or mixed with food and eaten.

The amount of THC is up to seven times greater in today's marijuana than in the mid-1980s product. This tremendous increase in potency is an unintended consequence of the efforts of law enforcement. Marijuana is very bulky when compared to the other illicit drugs, which increases the difficulty and risk of smuggling the product from the field to the user. Thus, producers have developed new, more powerful strains. This has made marijuana a more port-able, potent, and appealing drug, the exact opposite of the result intended by law enforcement.

Along with the trend toward more potent marijuana is the trend toward smaller plants developed by sophisticated horticultural methods. In the United States, marijuana grown indoors in forms that look more like bonsai plants than the large, traditional hemp plant has become a cash crop. It is possible to grow 100 of these plants in an area the size of a pool table. The DEA has estimated that the trend toward indoor growing has helped American growers increase the market share of home-grown, as compared to imported, marijuana from 12 percent in 1984 to 50 percent today.[47] Using high intensity "grow lights" and hydroponic and other high-tech growing methods indoors, growing is very difficult to detect. It is now pos-sible for a grower to control remotely by computer all the variables, such as temperature, moisture, and light. By equipping an indoor garden with sensors, a basic personal computer, and a modem, the grower can run the whole operation from afar. Thus, police may be able to find the garden but not the gardener.[48]

Another unintended consequence of the fight to eradicate mar-ijuana comes from the DEA's and others' use of paraquat, a poi-sonous chemical herbicide, to kill the plant. Sprayed from helicopters, the deadly chemical can lay waste to a field of marijuana in short order. However, growers have learned that if they harvest the plant quickly after it is sprayed, it retains its healthy appearance and can be readily sold — exposing the consumer to the unknown dan-gers of inhaling a highly toxic chemical. Some thoughtful legislators have proposed the inclusion of a distinctive color in paraquat to signal its presence, but to date nothing has been done.[49]

The use of marijuana is now so widespread that some cities and counties have softened their sanctions against the drug to the point that possession of small quantities is an often-ignored misdemeanor. By the early 1990s, 11 states had completely eliminated jail sentences for possession of a small amount of marijuana.[50] Other states continue to tilt at the marijuana windmill. Eric Single, of the Addiction Research Foundation in Toronto, said of limited legalization: "In those areas in which the effects of decriminalization were monitored, there appears to have been a minimal impact on rates of marijuana use, but a reduction in the social costs associated with the enforcement of the marijuana laws."[51]

Marijuana is particularly appealing to young people. It is perceived as a low-cost, relatively low-risk adventure. Typical of youth's attitude toward marijuana are these comments from a Gaithersburg, Maryland, boy. He said, "For me, marijuana is just like alcohol, no worse." The Partnership For a Drug Free America reported in 1998 that 71 percent of teenagers "Had friends who used" marijuana, and almost half admitted they had tried it themselves. In a student initiative at the University of Massachusetts, in 1993, a two-to-one vote favored the legalization of marijuana. U-Mass students forwarded the results to then-governor William Weld and asked him to instruct the university to cease arrests and prosecution of students for marijuana possession.[52] The governor demurred.

One of the major knocks on marijuana is that it causes otherwise productive, energetic people to become slothful and unmotivated. Evidence does not support that conclusion. Large numbers of successful, energetic people indulge with no external negative consequences other than the risk of legal sanctions.

Another common myth about marijuana is that it serves as a gateway to other drugs; that most cocaine users once smoked pot is offered as support for this position. Most heroin users once drank alcohol, but no one charges alcohol with being a gateway to heroin. The reason for this inconsistency is that marijuana does not enjoy the social acceptance of alcohol and is therefore a politically convenient target for such allegations. It may be that marijuana users are more likely than the population at large to use cocaine — because the black-market supply networks for the two drugs overlap. There is nothing in the pharmacology of marijuana that would make a user more or less likely to indulge in another substance.[53]

### Fear of Widespread Addiction Drives Fear of Legalization

Many argue against the legalization, or decriminalization, of drugs on the grounds that more people would become addicted than are addicted under the present prohibitionist laws. This theory, while politically popular, is inherently improbable and unsubstantiated. Within any group there will be a certain number prone to abuse of mind-altering substances. This propensity for abuse has everything to do with the individual's personal value system and psychological stability, and absolutely nothing to do with the legal status of drugs.

Those inclined to addictive behavior have that inclination independent of the law of the land, and have ample opportunity to obtain drugs under existing laws and customs. They currently have two major mind-altering alternatives available that are legal — prescription drugs and alcohol. A third alternative is illegal drugs. A slightly larger share (13 percent) of American households have used prescription-type psychotherapeutic drugs for nonmedical reasons than have used cocaine (12 percent).[54]

An individual inclined to escape reality through the medium of substance abuse will gravitate into that response to life whether or not the drugs used are legal. Legalizing currently illegal drugs will neither increase nor decrease the number of people inclined toward, or indulging in, addictive behavior.

An extensive household survey conducted in the early 1990s revealed that in the previous month, in 5 percent of the households someone had used marijuana, while less than 1 percent had used all other illicit drugs combined. This argues that alcohol, with its frequently cited 10 percent problematic usage, is a more troublesome social problem than cocaine, marijuana and heroin abuse combined.[55] If illicit drugs were legalized, some of the already addiction-prone population would migrate from alcoholism to drug abuse, and vice versa. But there is no reason to expect an increase in the number of people whose value systems or psychological profiles destine them to substance abuse.

## Addiction Can Be Cured

The poet and visionary William Blake, declared, "The road of excess leads to the palace of wisdom." Not so in his day or this day, unless the many addiction-fighting organizations now available could be interpreted as the palaces Blake had in mind. Phoenix House, founded in 1967, has become internationally known for its many drug treatment centers, and specializes in the use of the "therapeutic community" where groups of patients help and rely on each other. Other groups, such as Cocaine Anonymous, follow the "twelve-step program" approach of Alcoholics Anonymous that has had great success in leading to sobriety. As with all approaches to combating dependence and addiction, relapse is a major problem. It is, in fact, the most predictable element of the process.

Though advocates of twelve-step programs insist that a lifetime of abstinence is the only solution for an addict, several scientific studies have reported on addicts who have reverted from addiction to controlled use.[56] Certainly, once a person has visited the hell of addiction, lifelong abstinence is the safest course of action. However, to deny the possibility of controlled use for a former addict is to deny the truth, an element that is too frequently a casualty in the war on drugs.

That individuals can throw off an addiction is attested to by the 20 million Americans who quit smoking on their own in the decade between 1965 and 1975, even before the real public education campaign concerning the dangers of cancer and cardiovascular damage done by tobacco began.[57]

Stanton Peele, in *The Meaning of Addiction*, tells how the addict most effectively attacks addiction: "Addicts finally break out of the small world of addiction through combinations of changes in their external situations, . . . changes in their self-efficacy that enable them to achieve personal goals, and shifts in the reward value addicts attach to the addictive experience relative to their other values."[58]

Peele does not minimize the importance of treatment, but he emphasizes, as all thoughtful observers must, that responsibility for change rests with the user.

## Attitudes Change

Society's attitude toward the users of a particular drug, or drugs in general, changes over time, nor are attitudes about drugs consistent from one culture to the next. One culture's crime is another culture's sacrament.

The one constant regarding drugs is that every culture, during every age of mankind, has used them in one form or another. The single exception are the Eskimos: Because of their barren surroundings, they were unable to grow any substance-producing plants and consequently had to wait until fairly recently for the white man to introduce them to alcohol. Because of their culture's lack of experience with mind-altering substances, the results were legendary and devastating.

When coffee, which contains caffeine, was first introduced to Europe in the seventeenth century it was considered by the Roman Catholic church to be an evil substance. However, the church saw nothing wrong with the use of wine in religious and social rites. By contrast, some Muslims tolerate opium and marijuana but strictly forbid the use of alcohol.[59] The flower children of the 1960s provide a more contemporary example of inconsistent attitudes. They regarded the use of psychedelics and marijuana as beneficial, while many looked upon the use of alcohol with disdain.

On the other hand, there has always been consistency among some segment of any population that drug use is abhorrent.

## Facts Versus Myths

| Myth | Fact |
|---|---|
| 1. Drug users are mostly criminals preoccupied with stealing to buy drugs. | 1. The vast majority of illicit-drug users are otherwise law-abiding, productive citizens. |
| 2. Most people who use drugs become abusers. | 2. Fewer than 1 percent of those who try cocaine become daily users. |
| 3. Once an addict, always an addict. | 3. Many addicts are cured of their addiction. Some later return to controlled use. |
| 4. Heartless drug sellers recruit most new drug users. | 4. Most users are introduced to drugs by a friend who is often selling to support a habit. |
| 5. Many people die from using drugs. | 5. Eighty percent of drug deaths result from the illegality of drugs, not from the drugs themselves. |
| 6. Marijuana, cocaine and heroin are all addictive. | 6. Of the three major drugs, only heroin is truly addictive. Abuse of the others can create dependence but not addiction. |

Fighting the war on drugs with myths is a lot like hurling boomerangs at an enemy. They are unlikely to do the opponent any harm, and are likely to return to the throwers with devastating force.

# 2

# OTHER ILLEGAL DRUGS

How pleasant to fantasize that one day we will awake to the complete absence of marijuana, cocaine, and heroin from planet Earth. The world is still spinning. People still love, hate, and tolerate. Strength and weakness, stability and instability still exist in predictable inconsistency. For better or for worse, human nature continues to demand the ability to alter its consciousness. Nothing has really changed, except that of the countless herbs and chemicals available to achieve the mind's alteration, three previously available choices no longer exist. Is it then logical to assume that the removal of marijuana, cocaine, and heroin will make the world suddenly stop pursuing alteration of consciousness? No. What humans will do is find alternative means to achieve the same results. Even today, consciousness-altering alternatives to the Big Three are available.

Testifying before a congressional committee in 1994, the popular country singer Larry Gatlin, a former alcohol and drug abuser, warned:

> *If we stop every ounce of cocaine from coming into this country, if we stop every ounce of heroin from coming into this country, we had best call out the National Guard to guard every pharmacy, liquor store, beer joint and cocktail lounge in this country. Because if [people] want to feel better, they are going to find something to do it.*[1]

## Designer Drugs

Designer drugs such as Cat, Meth and PCP are produced by clandestine garage chemists whose technology allows them to design their own drugs from the endless array of available chemical combinations. The effects on humans are so similar to those of the well-known illicit drugs there is scarcely a difference. For a time, many designer drugs were actually legal because their chemical obscurity kept them from being included in the statutes as scheduled (illegal) drugs. As a result, the United States Congress hurriedly passed legislation — the Controlled Substance Analogue Control Act of 1986 — to outlaw any combination of drugs for human consumption, regardless of ingredients, which has structures or actions similar to those of a scheduled drug.[2]

## LSD

The father of designer drugs is LSD, or lysergic acid diethylamide. Among the world's most potent drugs, 25 micrograms of LSD can produce a "trip" of 10–12 hours. During the 1960s, LSD became a household term. Few people knew what the letters stood for, but many heard the blandishments of Harvard professor Timothy Leary about the wonderful worlds to be explored through this chemical medium. Some alleged that LSD was even celebrated in song by the Beatles in "Lucy in the Sky with Diamonds."

LSD was discovered in 1938 by a Swiss chemist, Albert Hofman, when he accidentally ingested some of the substance while experimenting with a fungus that attacks cereal grains. As a result of this chance encounter, he experienced vivid hallucinations, reporting "an intense kaleidoscopic play of colors."[3] Following this discovery, and some subsequent research, the Swiss pharmaceutical company for whom he worked began marketing LSD as a research drug throughout the world. It showed some promise for the treatment of specific forms of mental illness. But then the inevitable happened; knowledge of how to produce the drug fell into the hands of black-market profiteers, and LSD achieved widespread notoriety as *the* psychedelic drug of the 1960s. Echoing the sentiments of other well-intentioned chemists whose progeny have been corrupted into use as mind-altering substances, Mr. Hofman later referred to his discovery as "my problem child."[4]

LSD is usually taken by swallowing a tiny piece of blotter paper onto which the liquid chemical has been dropped. Other common methods are dropping it on a sugar cube, or into a glass of orange juice. In determining the length of a prison sentence for possessing LSD, until 1993 the weight of the blotter paper or sugar cube was included in the weight of the drug. As a result, $1,000 worth of LSD got a ten-year, no-parole sentence, the same sentence as $120,000 worth of heroin. "You've got kids serving ten years for a fraction of a gram of LSD," says Tom Hillier, the chief federal public defender in Seattle. "It doesn't survive the test of any civilized nation."[5] Judge Richard Posner labeled such decisions "looney," and exclaimed, "To base punishments on the weight of the carrier medium makes about as much sense as basing punishment on the weight of the defendant!"[6] In a unanimous 1996 decision the United States Supreme Court reaffirmed this lunacy in the case of *Neal vs. United States*, 94–9088. Justice Anthony M. Kennedy commented for the court that, while the logic of the law was flawed, it was up to Congress, not the judiciary, to rewrite bad laws. The issue illustrates the country's legal excesses as we seek the utopian objective of a drug-free society. Our chances of success would be no less should we legislate toward a society without sin.

After falling from favor during the 1970s and 1980s, LSD use has been increasing in recent years among students from the eighth to twelfth grades. The 1997 update of the annual University of Michigan study of drug use among schoolchildren showed that the number of tenth- and twelfth-graders who have tried LSD at least once has increased each year from 1992 through 1997, except for eighth graders between 1996 and 1997. For twelfth-graders, the 1997 figures showed an increase to 13.6 percent, from 8.6 percent in 1992.[7] Even more troubling, the same survey also reported a decrease in the negative perception the students had of LSD use.[8]

Some of this increasing popularity can be traced to economics.

The 10-to-12-hour trip referred to earlier can be achieved with a single dose of LSD costing $5 to $10. This compares to a crack cocaine high lasting 20 to 30 minutes for about the same cost. Ease of use is also a factor. To ingest LSD, all that's required is to swallow a tiny piece of innocuous blotter paper. Cocaine usually involves snorting, and crack requires a heat source and a pipe.

Another factor in the resurgence of LSD use is the simple passage of time. During LSD's heyday, many facts and rumors circulated about bad experiences with the drug. In the main, such bad trips were caused by lack of quality control and ignorance on the part of the people making and selling the drug, not to mention the users. These stories accumulated and contributed to LSD's decline. But today's teenagers were born in the 1980s, well after horror stories drove LSD from the psychedelic scene. Also, the increased knowledge and experience of today's illicit chemists means that LSD is of a much more even quality than in the past, and bad trips are rare.

## "Cat" Sneaks Up on the Drug Scene

The newest development in a long line of designer drugs is methcathinone, — street name, "cat." The drug was originally developed in the 1950s by a large American pharmaceutical company, but was shelved when its high potential for addiction and serious side effects were discovered.[9] An employee of the company had been instructed to destroy the old, unmarketable substance, but instead he started taking it to parties with friends from the University of Michigan.[10] It was never big in Ann Arbor, but it later surfaced on Michigan's somewhat remote Upper Peninsula in 1991 when some chemistry buffs figured out how to copy the formula. It soon became a home-brewed designer drug synthesized from easy-to-obtain household chemicals. Its use quickly spread to four adjoining states plus four others as far away as Washington. By mid-1994, 62 cat labs had been seized in those eight states with no discernible effect on the availability of the drug.[11] According to Don Simila, addiction rehabilitation supervisor at Michigan's Marquette Medical Clinic, "The potential for this to become a significant national problem does exist."12

Cat labs, where the drug is produced, are very simple, basic operations. Vans or motel rooms are the labs, making them difficult to find and shut down. The active ingredient in cat is ephedrine, an inexpensive, nonprescription stimulant used for weight loss and asthma control. It is processed with other easily obtained chemicals such as battery acid, Epsom salts, and drain cleaner. Cat is simple to synthesize and requires little chemical knowledge or training beyond obtaining the recipe, which has gotten much easier with its appearance on the Internet. And it is inexpensive. For an investment of about $500, a lab can create a batch of cat worth $50,000 on the street.13

Cat is said to produce a more intense, pleasurable high than cocaine but also has more side effects. It is either snorted or injected. According to the trade publication *Alcoholism and Drug Abuse Weekly*, "Sources agree that cat has made few inroads into the casual drug-user population. All of the cat addicts identified so far are considered hard-core drug users who had used a variety of drugs before discovering cat."14

Drug abusers readily migrate from one drug to another for a variety of reasons. If one drug becomes unavailable, abusers simply take up with another. This shines the harsh light of reality on the futility of interdiction. If the supply of this or that drug were cut off, demand, ingenuity, and greed would quickly supply a substitute.

## The Amphetamine Family

Amphetamines are the largest group of drugs from which designer-drug chemists draw their ingredients. From the amphetamine group of drugs that stimulate the central nervous system have come such well-known, legitimate products as Dexedrine, Benzedrine and Ritalin and such "street" drugs as speed, ice, ecstasy, and meth (street argot for methamphetamine). The common denominator of all these is the amphetamine molecule. Benzedrine was first synthesized as long ago as 1887, but was not used medically until 1932.[15] Because of the huge quantities of these drugs produced and consumed, they are relatively inexpensive. A producer of methamphetamine, a subset of the amphetamines, can cook up $50,000 worth of the stuff, at wholesale, for an investment of $4,000 in chemicals and a day's work.[16] Methamphetamines are not a new phenomenon: It is documented that Adolph Hitler was a "speed freak."[17] And according to University of California–Los Angeles psychopharmacologist, Ronald K. Siegel, John F. Kennedy was given methamphetamine injections by his personal physician before important summit meetings.[18]

Meth is currently the fastest-growing designer drug in both production and use. Testifying before a congressional committee, Administrator Thomas A. Constantine of the U.S. Drug Enforcement Agency (DEA) said in 1994, "Methamphetamine, also known as 'speed' and 'crank,' is the most significant dangerous drug problem in terms of domestic clandestine manufacture and widespread distribution."[19]

In general, the effects that amphetamines produce and their means of ingestion are very similar to cocaine's except that the resulting high lasts much longer. The effects of cocaine last 20 to 30 minutes, whereas amphetamines stimulate the body for at least four hours. A systematic, scientific research program, the results of which were published in the March 1982 issue of *Scientific American*, found that regular cocaine users were unable to distinguish between the effects of cocaine and amphetamines.[20]

## The Synthetic Anesthetics

PCP, or phencyclidine hydrochloride, is a widely used synthetic drug, originally developed as an anesthetic. Unlike ether, it did not make patients unconscious, but rather put them into a state of dissociation from their bodies. It allowed them to undergo surgical procedures without any awareness of pain. After two years the drug was withdrawn from medical use because of too many reported incidents of mental and visual disturbances following its use.[21] Shortly thereafter it appeared on the black market.

PCP's effect on the user is much like that of the opiate morphine, from which heroin is derived. Professor Randy E. Barnett of the Illinois Institute of Technology and a former prosecutor for the Illinois state's attorney's office, makes this observation:

> Drug laws make ... opiates artificially scarce and thereby create a powerful (black) market incentive for clandestine chemists to develop alternative "synthetic" drugs that can be made more cheaply and with less risk of detection by law enforcement. The hallucinogen phencyclidine hydrochloride — or "PCP" — is one drug that falls into this category.[22]

The powdered form of PCP, angel dust, can be sprinkled on marijuana cigarettes to enhance their effect. It is also frequently snorted like cocaine.

## Alternative Drugs: An Unintended Consequence

The harm being done to America by our drug problem results not only from the drugs themselves but from the many unintended consequences of poorly conceived public policy.

The ultimate unintended consequence of the drug war has been the creation of innumerable alternative drugs, only a few of which we have discussed. Their development has been a direct and economically inevitable response to the artificially high black-market prices commanded by the mainstream illicit drugs. Should the United States succeed in stopping the flow of any or all of the three big drugs — marijuana, cocaine, and heroin — production of existing alternatives would immediately and dramatically accelerate, as would the development of new and "better" alternative ways to alter consciousness. The number of people who would seek chemical alteration of their moods would not decline; these people would simply seek out available products that work best for them.

This inevitable response should be called the Law of Unintended Consequences, and hewn onto a grand portico or cornerstone:

> *Whenever government imposes prohibition on the sale of a commodity for which a substantial demand exists, the immutable laws of the marketplace will cause unintended, undesirable consequences to ensue. The negative impact of these consequences will far outweigh any positive results of that prohibition.*

# 3

━━━━◦◦◦◦◦━━━━

# MONEY IS INDEED THE ROOT
# OF THIS EVIL

*Of all the foul growths current in the world, the worst is money. Money drives men from home, plunders proud cities, and perverts honest minds to shameful practice, godlessness and crime.*

SOPHOCLES

We presume when Sophocles wrote "money," he meant inordinate profits or greed, and in that context, his words are relevant to the intractability of the drug problem today. The former attorney general of Colombia, Dr. Gustavo de Greiff, has stated:

*What is surprising is that it has taken so long for the central fact of the drug trade to sink in: As long as a kilo of cocaine changes in value from $500 to perhaps $20,000 by virtue of the short flight from Colombia to the United States, there will always be people who will be willing to enter the business. . . . Our present approach offers criminals, large and small, a profit margin that no honest business ordinarily yields. In the process we . . . contribut[e] to the generation of all the problems and vices that accompany drugs, i.e., violence, corruption, and a generalized disregard for law.*[1]

To fully grasp the outlandish price levels to which illicit drugs have been inflated by prohibition, we need only compare them to the recent trading price of gold, which is well established and published each day. Such a comparison reveals the relative amounts people are willing to pay for one commodity (gold), whose value is the very definition of "intrinsic," and others, whose value is completely dubious.

| Commodity | Price per ounce (dollars) |
|-----------|:-------------------------:|
| Pure gold | 312 |
| Pure heroin | 28,000 |
| Cocaine | 3,900 |
| Marijuana | 300 |

About one out of every three Americans has paid those prices for illicit drugs one or more times in his or her life.[2] According to the Office of National Drug Control Policy, a total of over $57 billion is spent on illicit drugs each year.[3]

## The Other Intoxicant In Cocaine

As in any business, the producers of cocaine try to keep their costs to a minimum. What makes the drug business so intoxicatingly profitable is the black-market price compared to the minuscule cost of production. According to Peter Reuter, former head of Rand Corporation's drug study group, "The cost of growing coca leaves and refining them into cocaine constitute an absolutely trivial share of the cost of cocaine to American consumers."[4]

The small share of drug profits that go to the growers and processors is clearly demonstrated by Dr. de Greiff's example of the profit from a kilo of cocaine. In fact, the kilos street value can range from $15,000 to as much as $40,000, depending on the American city. That huge margin goes directly into the pocket of the Colombian cartel that bought the drug in Colombia and smuggled it into the United States.

To put that kind of profit-generating power into perspective, let's assume that 100,000 kilos of cocaine are smuggled into the

United States each year (no one really knows the exact amount). Using the low price of $15,000 and subtracting the $500-per-kilo production cost would yield $14,500 in gross profit per kilo. If we multiply that per-kilo profit by the estimated 100,000 kilos, the gross profit to cocaine smugglers alone is nearly *$1.5 billion* per year.

On most legal products, a Colombian exporter would be happy with a gross profit of 20 to 100 percent of his $500 cost, depending on the product. For 100,000 kilos, the production cost would be $50,000,000, and a 20-to-50-percent normal profit structure would produce gross profits of $10,000,000 to $50,000,000 a year. When this is compared to the nearly $1.5 billion generated by cocaine, the term "obscene profits" begins to define itself.

The kilo of cocaine for which the United States importer has paid $15,000 is broken into the usual quarter-gram dosage units, 12,500 per kilo; they would sell for $10 each in many markets. That turns our $15,000 kilo into $125,000. Again, most importers would be delighted with a 100 percent markup, in this case $30,000. Compare that to the 833 percent markup of selling a kilo of cocaine retail.

The preceding description is a highly simplified version of what usually takes place in the illicit drug market. Frequently there are several levels of dealers between the smuggler and the user. Having many links in the distribution chain is important to those higher up, because it affords them insulation in case someone below runs afoul of the law. But these many levels exact a terrible price from the users because at each level the risk taker must be compensated by huge profits. If a kilo of cocaine is imported for $15,000, and its price is doubled in each of six succeeding levels of distribution, the resulting value is $960,000. This, plus the dilution that can take place several times on the way to the user, accounts for the multiplications of the original cost that result in the multi-million-dollar estimates of street value.

Smugglers deal in multi-kilo, sometimes multi-ton, shipments of cocaine. The cocaine can then be broken down to individual kilo dealers, pound dealers, and even ounce, gram and part-gram dealers. Each takes a profit based on what the market will bear.

## Heroin Weighs Less, Costs More

Heroin has a capacity even greater than cocaine for the generation of disgusting profits. In our cocaine example, a kilo had a value in the source country of $500 and a wholesale value upon arrival in the United States of $15,000. A kilo of heroin, on the other hand, has a value in the Far East of about $5,000 and a wholesale value in the United States of perhaps $250,000, depending on city and market conditions. The kilo of cocaine sold retail for $125,000, while the kilo of heroin would command perhaps $1,000,000. Actual prices vary widely, but these estimates serve to provide a comparison between heroin and cocaine.

The difference in value per kilo between cocaine and heroin is mainly because an average dose of heroin is much smaller. To the dealer, smuggling a million dollars' worth of heroin requires moving less than 10 percent as much product as with cocaine, resulting in much less risk.

## Marijuana: A Huge Cash Crop

The marijuana market is very different from the cocaine and heroin markets. The production and distribution of cocaine and heroin are characterized by importation from a foreign producer at relatively low costs, followed by distribution through a multilevel distribution network that accounts for most of the final retail price. Marijuana's distribution is much less formalized. A substantial part of what is produced domestically is for personal use or is sold to immediate friends or family. For the imported product, the chain of distribution has fewer links than cocaine and heroin. Because of the growth of domestic production, the proportion of U.S. marijuana consumption smuggled in from outside (mainly from Mexico and the Orient) has fallen below 50 percent.

No figures on the cost of marijuana production in the United States are available. However, it can be assumed to be comparable to other relatively simple crops. A stand of 300 mature plants can produce marijuana worth $1,000,000 (wholesale) per annual harvest.[5] Some hydroponic growers can coax two, or even three, harvests per year from their pampered plants.

Wholesale marijuana prices are normally quoted by the pound. We quote them here by the ounce to provide a convenient basis for comparison. As with the other major drugs, prices vary widely by quality and location. The wholesale price can range from $30 for some cheap Mexican offerings, heavy with stalks and stems, to $300 per ounce for a pure, high-grade, American-grown product.

Retail marijuana prices vary greatly from one city to another. New York City prices are somewhat high and range from $100 to as much as $600 per ounce.[6] By comparison, a standard package of 20 cigarettes contains one ounce of tobacco and retails for around $2. And cigarette companies must assume the costs of production of the tobacco, the filter, the package, and the taxes assessed by multiple levels of government, plus the costs associated with the advertising and promotion of cigarettes. Growers, importers and sellers of marijuana have no such overhead, resulting in the extravagant profits that lure so many into its production and distribution.

## There Is No Honor Among Thieves (or Drug Dealers)

With the exception of marijuana, all illicit drugs are "cut," or diluted, one or more times in the process of production and distribution. The amount and methods of dilution vary, but the motive is consistent: to make more money. Dilution directly impacts profitability because the diluents are inexpensive, hopefully inert ingredients such as lactose, inositol, or mannitol, added only to increase the profit per gram to the dealer.

Cocaine from the producer ranges in purity from 70 to 90 percent. According to DEA figures, the average purity of cocaine seized on the streets dropped from 72 percent in 1987 to 54 percent in 1990. It then rose to 61 percent by 1995.[7]

Heroin is similarly cut, or "stepped on," in street parlance. With its higher potency, heroin can withstand greater amounts of dilution than cocaine and still produce a satisfactory result. Heroin of less than 10 percent purity was once commonplace in the black market. During the mid- and late-1990s, heroin purity has risen dangerously and unpredictably. Purity above 70 percent is now common in both New York City and Philadelphia.[8]

## The Irony of Drug Purity

The drug war, while barren of results, is rich in ironies. Increased law enforcement pressure on drug smuggling has encouraged greater purity of product, since less dilution means less bulk, which results in a reduced chance of discovery. As law enforcement pressure increases, drug smugglers constantly seek drugs of greater potency per pound. Greater purity helps keep weight, thus discovery and prosecution, down. The risks are less and the profits the same.[9]

Some recent samples of heroin have reached above 70 percent purity. Many observers feel that the increase in demand for heroin is due to the drug's increased purity. Heroin purity above 70 percent makes snorting or smoking the drug practical, whereas lower-purity heroin is only efficient and cost-effective when injected, with all the attendant risks of the needle.

When we enact policies that encourage higher-purity drugs, we are ignoring the increased-potency lesson that we learned with the prohibition of alcohol. During Prohibition, the consumption of lower-potency alcoholic beverages, such as beer, plummeted while the market share of moonshine and other strong distilled spirits soared.[10] Soon after the repeal of Prohibition, the consumer patterns for both high- and low-potency beverage consumption returned to pre-Prohibition levels.[11] We can extrapolate from this that the shift to more potent drugs is directly related to the prohibition of drugs. This conclusion is strengthened by the decline in potency of today's legal drugs. Unfiltered cigarettes have given way to the lower-nicotine, filtered brands. Decaffeinated coffee is gaining market share at the expense of regular coffee, and hard liquor has declined in popularity while beer and wine sales have increased.

## The "Crime Tax"

Contributing mightily to the profitability of illicit-drug dealing is a factor sometimes referred to as the "crime tax." When a person engages in illegal activity with risks involved, he expects it to pay more than legitimate work. Chances of apprehension, conviction, jail time to be served if convicted, and the risks to life and limb of associating with criminals, all contribute to determining the amount of the "tax."

For example, when a sealed, one-ounce bottle of pharmaceutical cocaine worth about $50 in legitimate commerce was stolen, it immediately commanded $3,200 on the black market.[12] The value differential was due entirely to its illegal status — a modern version of Merlin's magic — taking relatively inexpensive chemicals and transforming them into treasure by waving the wand of prohibition. As Steven Wisotsky, in his book *Beyond the War on Drugs*, put it:

> *If the cocaine industry commissioned a consultant to design a mechanism to ensure its profitability, it could not have done better than the war on drugs: just enough pressure to inflate prices from $2 to $100 per gram, but not enough to keep its product from the market.*
>
> *This is the stubborn paradox of prohibition: by arti-*

*ficially inflating prices, the laws against drug dealing create opportunities for instant wealth. The criminal law thus institutionalizes its own violation, accompanied by a corrosive set of black market pathologies.*[13]

The Armed Forces are not the only institutions that recruit. Because illegal drugs are so enormously expensive, most regular users need help in paying for their indulgence. Dr. Carol Boyd, of the University of Michigan, conducted a study of 105 women with a crack cocaine habit. She determined that each spent an average of $672 per week on the drug.[14] A Florida study puts the figure at a minimum of $350 per week.[15] The cost of abusing drugs is a substantial item on the budget of all but the most affluent. To help pay for their habits, many users turn to selling drugs. In fact, 70 percent of those who deal drugs are also users.[16]

Most people are introduced to drugs by friends, often due to a strong financial incentive. Each person introduced to drug use provides the seller with another source of income. What results is the drug market's version of a Mary Kay network. Legalization, with its attendant lowering of prices to something more closely resembling a normal business markup, would eliminate the financial incentive for user/sellers to recruit more users.

## The Irresistible Lure of Easy Money

Many dealers are in the business because they see it as their only way out of seemingly hopeless circumstances. A 16-year-old from Washington, D.C., virtually unemployable after having been arrested 12 times, manages to clear the heady sum of $300 to $400 a day selling crack. "I don't want to make this a life thing," he alleges, "I'll quit when I get out of high school." He then makes a telling and contradictory admission: "But when you start you really can't stop. The money is too good."[17]

A Baltimore man who had been laid off for two and a half years from his $24.60-per-hour job as a steelworker was unable to find comparable pay in any legitimate employment. He went into the illicit-drug business as a "runner," delivering $2,000 per day worth of $10 heroin packets, and now makes an adequate living from his share of the daily collections.[18] His refusal to turn to legitimate entry-level work is not unusual. One young drug dealer said, only half in jest, that drug dealing was the only service job available where you don't have to wear a funny hat. Phillippe Bourgois, an anthropologist who has studied drug trafficking in East Harlem, writes, "Compared to earning chump change working for the white man at McDonald's, the drug trade can seem more realistic and even noble."[19]

Vast numbers of low-level crack dealers and marijuana peddlers of all races from America's inner cities share, to varying degrees, the cheerless circumstances of the laid-off steelworker and the unemployable 16-year-old. In terms of sheer numbers, they make up most of the army of drug dealers who supply the nation's users.

Bourgois observed: "Crack has created a new Horatio Alger myth for inner-city kids searching for meaning and upward mobility. It's really their American dream."[20]

## The Entrepreneurial Dealer and Life in the Fast Lane

The huge monetary rewards of the drug business draw some very capable people into drug dealing, people capable enough to make it in legitimate business. Gustavo, born and raised in Colombia, attended university at Bogotá, where he earned a degree in physics. He planned to start his own legitimate business but needed money to get established, so he joined a Colombian smuggling operation coordinating shipments to Miami. He felt he could make a large amount of money in a short time and then get out. He explains:

> *There's a weird phenomenon that takes control of everyone that ever gets into this business. You start out with a plan to make some money so that you can do something legal. You tell*

*yourself, "I'm only going to do this for a short time." But once you get in you can't get out. Something forces you to keep going. The money, the excitement, the feel of incredible wealth — all of that comes into play. The business pulls you and pulls you. Once you start running major loads, there's no escape. It's exhilarating.*[21]

The truly entrepreneurial drug dealer, like his counterpart in legitimate business, is always looking for a way to better his situation. Many who start out as street dealers move on to become "weight buyers" — dealers who buy in kilo or multi-kilo amounts and break it down for others to sell at retail. Dealers who graduate to this level can leverage their efforts through the work of others, which, after all, is what entrepreneurship is all about. Because the profits from drug dealing are so huge and easily garnered, greed, that ignoble motivation of *Homo sapiens,* takes over.

Ponder the words of a young man who began dealing drugs as a vulnerable teenager:

*Money is like a drug. Once you get a little taste of it you want more. And when you start getting a whole lot of it you still want more. It's like a fever. An addiction. There ain't no such thing as enough. . . . I first started selling drugs when I was thirteen. I was working for this guy that drove a flashy Corvette. He was my role model, and he got me into the business. By the time I was fifteen, I was doing ten thousand dollars' worth of business every day selling cocaine, heroin, BAM and dust. Out of that ten thousand my take would be twenty-five hundred. That's a lot of money for a little teenage boy to be bringing in every day.*[22]

Judging by the flamboyant lifestyle adopted by some drug dealers, one could argue that they are drawn to the business by the realization that only with the easy money of illicit drugs could they ever indulge their fantasies. They do double damage to the fabric of society, first by importing and selling their drugs and then by becoming role models for young people, many of whom aspire to the same display of conspicuous consumption.

Opulent examples of high-flying, flamboyant drug dealers abound in south Florida. Home to some of the most successful powerboat racers in the country, it is also home to several participants who are able to afford their hobby only because of the vast sums they have made in the drug trade. Armando "Mandy" Fernandez was crowned North American champion of the offshore powerboat circuit and named Boater of the Year by *The Miami Herald* in 1991. Four years later he pleaded guilty to an indictment that he smuggled 6,000 pounds of cocaine and 30,000 pounds of marijuana from Colombia into the United States through the Bahamas. The proceeds from his smuggling activities financed his boat-racing campaigns and his string of luxury foreign car dealerships. Known as "The Collection," they included Jaguar, Porsche, and Ferrari. He also purchased and ran a night club and invested heavily in luxury ocean-front condominiums with his estimated $16 million in drug profits.[23]

## Q: How Does One Clean Up Drug Money So It Can Be Spent? A: Launder It.

Because drug selling is illegal, it is conducted almost entirely with cash; no checks, no credit cards, just greenbacks, please. This presents the sellers of any substantial quantity of drugs with a real problem. They can hardly spend or bank their huge amounts of cash without its source being obvious. Imagine the suspicions raised if a person walked into a car dealership with a suitcase full of cash to buy a new car, or if a buyer of real estate showed up to close escrow with $200,000 in $20 bills.

The very volume of transactions and the amount of cash generated pose some daunting logistical problems for large drug dealers.

U.S. drug sales generate over $50 billion per year, almost entirely in cash, and $1 million in $20 bills weighs over 100 pounds. A startling example of the pure bulk of this cash is provided by a single U.S. Customs Service seizure of $22 million in drug proceeds; the more than 900,000 individual bills weighed 3,000 pounds.[24]

The need of drug dealers to clean up criminally large amounts of cash gave rise to the growth and sophistication of money laundering, the attempt to conceal illegal cash or other income by converting it to other assets. For example, the Colombian cartels launder hundreds of millions in drug money each year by using it to purchase household appliances in the United States for shipping home to be sold, often at prices ruinous to legitimate Colombian appliance dealers.

Official estimates of the volume of U.S. money laundering range from $10 billion to more than $100 billion per year. Those who participate in this shadowy business are paid from .025 percent to one percent for simply being couriers of the cash. Even that small percentage can earn a courier between $2,500 and $10,000 for carrying $1 million from one place to another. The primary launderers who actually transfer the cash through the banking system keep 4 to 6 percent of what they handle.[25]

To help the authorities detect illicit activity such as drug dealing or income tax evasion, the Bank Secrecy Act was passed in 1970; it requires that any cash transaction of $10,000 or more be reported to the government. Initially, this law was weakly enforced and was widely ignored as an intrusion of privacy and unnecessary paperwork burden on banks. Its intent and effectiveness were reinforced by the Money Laundering Control Act of 1986, which made the act of money laundering per se illegal and punishable by fines or imprisonment or both.

## One Can Go to Jail for Helping with the Laundry

Many money launderers have gone to jail, and organizations have paid millions of dollars in fines for breaking the money-laundering laws, yet some still see laundering as a technicality rather than a moral issue. Some otherwise good and honorable organizations and individuals who wouldn't go near an actual drug transaction see little wrong with laundering money — until they find themselves mired in deep legal trouble.

In 1994, a subsidiary of the venerable American Express Company, while admitting no wrong-doing, paid $14 million in fines and forfeitures and wrote off a $19 million loan to an alleged drug dealer (clearing the way for the Feds to seize the collateral). This was part of a settlement with the Justice Department of a civil case and came after two employees of American Express Bank International had been found guilty in a criminal case of helping an alleged Mexican drug dealer launder $30 million through the bank's Beverly Hills, California branch.[26]

The lure of money laundering to those not usually associated with criminal activity is illustrated by a 1994 New York City case that culminated in the arrest of some seemingly solid citizens. Among those arrested on charges of laundering more than $100 million were an honorary consul general for the Republic of Bulgaria, a firefighter, a policeman, a lawyer, a hospital administrator, a stockbroker, and two rabbis.[27] Commenting on the arrest of the laundering ring, New York FBI head, William A. Gavin, said, "Money became the narcotic. It shows the pervasive influence of narcotics in our society." Collaborating on the case, Carlo A. Boccia of the DEA said the defendants had a common motivation, "greed, a true example of how drug profits do corrupt at all levels of society."[28]

In addition to domestic money laundering, there are relentless efforts by foreign smugglers to sneak their illicit profits out of the United States. Smuggling currency out of the country has become so prevalent that authorities have turned to the same interception methods used to staunch the flow of illicit drugs into the country. Assisted by drug-sniffing dogs and other techniques, the Customs Service seizes from smugglers an average of over $40 million per year in unreported currency. An inspection of outgoing cargo turned up over $7 million in cash in one shipment of dried peas bound for Colombia.[29]

A case tried in federal court in Los Angeles demonstrates that stopping the export of foreign drug profits is as much a Sisyphean struggle for our nation as our efforts to cut off importation of the drugs themselves. A laundering ring was arrested that had smuggled more than $50 million in drug profits to Bolivia in a two-year period. The smugglers used various household appliances as containers for the cash, including freezers, vacuum cleaners, and stereo equipment. "We could hide about $200,000 in one speaker," a member of the smuggling ring revealed.[30] From the New York City area comes a report of alert customs inspectors who found $6 million of drug money in refrigerated cannisters used to ship bull semen, $1 million in pallets containing boxes of strawberries, and $14 million hidden in the cores of massive spools of cable.[31] Short of dismantling every piece of furniture and equipment the United States exports, there is simply no way to stop the flow of drug profits out of our country.

## A New Kind of Nuclear Threat

The existence of billions of criminally controlled dollars and the economic power they confer has caused concern to leaders around the world. They fear that newly dismantled Soviet nuclear weapons or some of their key components could fall into the hands of drug-enriched criminal enterprises.

Several reports have surfaced of the smuggling and sale of weapons-grade fissionable material.[32] North Korea is a nation that has shown a terrifying tendency to develop its nuclear program. One major hurdle it faces is the acquisition of hard currency with which to finance its nuclear aspirations. Disturbing reports have circulated of trafficking in heroin between North Korea and Russia, including a recent $1 million seizure of North Korean heroin near Vladivostok. Diplomats, international security officials, and western intelligence agencies have all expressed concern that North Korea could turn to drug trafficking as a means of raising hard currency.[33] Other rogue countries present and future would have no compunctions about acquiring money through drug trafficking to enhance their nuclear ambitions. The huge profit margin of illicit drugs has the potential to finance nuclear terrorism even as it finances social pathologies here at home.

# 4

---

# SOCIETAL HARM FROM
# DRUG MONEY

## Corruption Is the Cancer, Money the Carcinogen

The corruption of public officials — police, judges, border and prison guards, customs inspectors, and others in positions of public trust — is a corrosive consequence of our prohibitionist drug policies, and a nationwide problem. The disastrous drug decades of the 1970s and 1980s saw the number of federal convictions of public officials increase from 44 in 1970 to 1067 in 1988.[1] When the hundreds of convictions of state and local police and other officials are added in, the true magnitude of the problem is apparent.

This kind of wholesale law-breaking in America could only result from a breakdown in respect for drug laws. Although our ingrained respect for law and order causes us to slam on the brakes at a red light, even at four in the morning, with no one in sight, our drug laws lack the moral suasion necessary to command such broad adherence. In this area of shaky moral consensus, breaking drug laws can be easily rationalized by public officials of marginal character. We learned that lesson during alcohol Prohibition; our national amnesia destines us to re-learn it.

The following vignette, related by a drug smuggler to a U.S. Senate investigator, illustrates the enormous wealth and potential for corruption created by the drug business.

> *One night after we'd gotten several loads [of drugs] in we brought in all these duffel bags full of money. We started dumping them on the floor, and pretty soon the entire floor in*

*the living room — wall to wall — was covered with money.*
*We were standing knee-deep in twenty-dollar bills. This was*
*a big living room. We're talking about millions of dollars of*
*cash lying on the floor. Most people can't even imagine what*
*it's like to be standing knee-deep in a couple of million dollars.*
*How many times can you expose yourself to that and not give*
*in to temptation?*

*That's why there is so much corruption among law en-*
*forcement people involved in the drug war. Cops will bust a*
*place, and one of them will find thousands of dollars stashed*
*away in a back room. He'll grab a handful and stuff it in his*
*pocket. He knows that what he grabs in that one handful will*
*be more than his salary for the entire month. He also knows*
*that nobody will be doing any counting until he turns the*
*money in.*[2]

Bribery corrupts far and wide. A member of law enforcement
can provide protection against arrest in exchange for a periodic cash
payment. An arrested drug dealer can buy his way out of the charge
by offering a bribe on the spot. A cash-laden defendant can purchase
perjured testimony or bribe a judge. Less blatant but no less effective
is the submission by the arresting officer of an intentionally flawed
report, which opens the door for the defense to declare that evidence
was illegally obtained. Border guards and customs inspectors are also
vulnerable to bribery. In one five-year conspiracy, allegedly responsible for moving some $78 million worth of cocaine through the
Calexico border crossing, an Immigration and Naturalization Service border guard and a Customs Service inspector were charged
with accepting between $30,000 and $50,000 per load to pass shipments of cocaine through the gateway. More than a dozen other
inspectors and supervisors were reportedly under investigation in the
case.[3] The difficulty in preventing this type of corruption is under-
scored by the modest government salaries of those charged —
around $45,000 per year.

A small mid-1990s nationwide sampling of drug-related corruption cases of our public officials provides more evidence of the breadth and depth of the problem:

• Nine New Orleans police officers were indicted on drug charges. A federal prosecutor called corruption within the police department "rampant and systemic." During the FBI sting operation, agents paid the police more than $97,000 in bribes. It was estimated that as many as 20 additional officers could have been implicated if the operation had not been curtailed after the initial arrests to protect the identities of undercover agents.[4]

• In 1993, for the fifth time in four years, police arrested Washington, D.C., prison guards on charges of taking bribes and smuggling drugs into the prisons they were paid to protect. About 40 guards and other D.C. prison employees were charged with bribery or drug violations during those four years.[5]

• One of the largest cases of drug-related police corruption in U.S. history came to a belated conclusion in 1994 when the last two fugitive officers of a group of more than 100 Miami, Florida, officers surrendered to the FBI. Labeled the "Miami River Cops," they had been arrested, fired or disciplined for stealing cocaine from smugglers and reselling it. One had been hiding for eight years in Puerto Rico, the other in Colombia.[6]

• In the largest case of police corruption in California history, after five years of investigations, arrests and prosecutions 29 deputies from the Los Angeles County Sheriff's Department were convicted of stealing drug money. Most of those convicted admitted to skimming millions of dollars from various drug busts during the middle and late 1980s. Some also admitted to planting evidence, filing false reports, abusing suspects, and perjuring themselves. The total amount of cash the deputies stole will never be known, but one deputy admitted to helping steal $800,000 in a single raid. Another officer admitted that in a period of about three years, he personally pocketed more than $500,000. According to another, on more than one occasion two deputies scooped cash from a drug operation into bags and boxes, hid it from their honest colleagues, and divided it up in the squad car as soon as they were alone.

What made Operation Big Spender, as it was called, all the more tragic was the prior sterling records of at least two of its leaders. Robert Sobel, the highly regarded sergeant of the elite group of antidrug operatives known as the major narcotics team, was the first to come forward and admit that he and others were stealing money. He was admired by some as culpable but courageous, and vilified by others as a bad cop who ratted to save his own skin. Another key player, Eufrasio "Al" Cortez, had won the prestigious Officer of the Year award from the California Narcotic Officers Association a few years earlier, as well as a bravery citation after being wounded in the line of duty. Obviously, these men could have had distinguished careers in law enforcement if not for their inability to resist the temptation of quick and easy drug money. As the *Los Angeles Times* put it: "Seeing themselves as unsung, underpaid warriors, they stole." The drug money bought otherwise unaffordable boats, recreational vehicles, vacation homes in Arizona, helicopter lessons and even a part interest in a racehorse. The team threw a lavish party for itself at the posh Ritz-Carlton in the Southern California seaside village of Dana Point. To top off the evening, one deputy proudly displayed a new revolver with dollar signs engraved on its pearl handle and a jewel-encrusted barrel.[7]

Providing a summary of the seriousness of drug money corruption, a front-page article in the *Washington Post* entitled "In Drug War, Crime Sometimes Wears a Badge," described . . .

> *. . . a growing national wave of corruption, as one group of police officers after another in major cities across the country succumb to the temptations of the illegal drug trade. In the District of Columbia, 77 officers face criminal charges. . . . The former police chiefs of Detroit, Michigan and Rochester, N.Y., have been convicted on drug related charges, and department-wide drug scandals have hit Philadelphia,*

*Miami, Cleveland and Los Angeles as well as small towns along the southern Atlantic coastal region favored by drug smugglers."*[8]

And so the cancer spreads. And the spreading will continue until the cause is excised. Until the United States removes the profit from the drug trade, those profits will continue to buy vulnerable public officials. Fortunately for our society, the vast majority of law enforcement people are honest men and women who wear the shield of public trust with honor and dignity. Still, a significant number succumb to the combination of weak moral fiber, modest incomes, and the availability of huge amounts of easy money.

## Drug Money Destabilizes Other Countries

Several drug-financed dramas of Shakespearean proportions, played out simultaneously in Mexico and Colombia, illustrate how narco-dollars, as our neighbors to the south refer to drug money, exacerbate already serious social and economic problems.

Carlos Salinas, Mexico's former president, was highly regarded on both sides of the border while in office. He was a major factor in forging the North American Free Trade Agreement (NAFTA) between Mexico and the U.S. In 1994 his brother, Rauel, was indicted for allegedly planning and financing the murder of José Massieu, the secretary general of Mexico's ruling party, P.R.I. Mexican authorities alleged that Rauel Salinas had funneled more than $300,000 to a conspirator in the murder.[9] Shortly after the murder, a confessed accomplice was quoted in the press as saying that "the money to pay for the murder of José Massieu came from a man with ties to a major Mexican drug-smuggling cartel."[10]

In 1996, Leobardo Larios Guzman, the courageous former chief prosecutor of Mexico's Jalisco state, was assassinated, gangland style. According to Jorge Lopez Vergara, who replaced Guzman in the Jalisco post, Guzman had conducted several investigations into the Mexican drug cartels during his term in office, including heading up the investigation of the death of Cardinal Juan Jesus Posados Ocampo, gunned down at Guadalajara Airport in 1994. Commenting on Guzman's assassination, Vergara said, "It has to do with Larios' having acted with honesty and firmness in those investigations."[11] Mexico's federal attorney, General Antonio Lozano, was even more explicit. He said, "Some of the people we have found to have participated in the murder [of Guzman] are linked with the homicide of Cardinal Posadas Ocampo."[12]

## Colombia Suffers From Too Much Drug Money

While there is no shortage of honest and courageous policemen and judges in Colombia, neither is there a shortage of those on the take. U.S. Officials estimated that toward the end of his career, the late Colombian cartel leader Pablo Escobar spent $1 million per day just to stay out of jail.[13] That money didn't go to the tooth fairy; it went to policemen, prosecutors, judges, the military, and others in positions of public trust who could help protect Escobar.

Writing in *Foreign Policy*, Princeton Professor Ethan Nadelmann succinctly sums up the effect of narco-dollars throughout Central and South America:

> *Government officials ranging from common police officers to judges to cabinet ministers have been offered bribes many times their annual government salaries, and often for doing nothing more than looking the other way. In addition, the limits on what can be bought with corruption have evaporated. Supreme court judges, high-ranking police and military officers, and cabinet officers are no longer above such things. The ultimate degree of corruption is when government officials take the initiative in perpetrating crimes. This has occurred not just in the major drug-producing countries but throughout*

*the continent as well. No country, from Cuba to Chile, seems to be immune.*[14]

The drug-related corruption that so permeates not only Mexico and Colombia but also other South American countries is a direct result of the gush of drug dollars from the United States. Regardless of where they happen to change hands, these monies owe their existence to and have their origins in the United States. Some would say that this puts too much blame on the United States, that other countries buy illicit drugs as well. And they do, but if, by legalization, we put a stop to the profits of illegal drug selling in America, other countries would possibly follow our lead.

## Trade Unfettered by Law Begets Violence

America abounds with legitimate industries locked in the daily combat we call competition. For all its ferocity, it is conducted, for the most part, within the constraints of the law. When the rules are broken or bad-faith bargaining occurs, the antagonists go to court to seek redress for wrongs real and imagined. The illicit-drug business provides a violent contrast to civilized commerce, because there is no mechanism to settle the inevitable conflicts of the marketplace except the use of violence. When a buyer fails to pay what is owed, the seller's only recourse is the law of the jungle.

Separate studies compiled between 1988 and 1991 of homicides in New York City, Washington, D.C., and Miami showed that 24 to 35 percent were drug-related and that more than 70 percent of the drug-related homicides were "systemic" rather than being caused by the actual use of a drug.[15] One such study reported:

*Seventy-four percent of all New York's drug-related homicides and 85 percent of crack-related homicides were systemic, that is, they stemmed from the exigencies of working or doing* *business in a black market rather than from either the economic compulsivity of addicts or the psychopharmacological effects of the drugs. Interestingly, of the 31 drug-related homicides that were determined to be psychopharmacological, crack accounted for only three (<10 percent), while alcohol accounted for 21 (67 percent).*[16]

From New York City comes a report of the arrest of a gang of 48 suspected drug dealers from the Upper West Side of Manhattan who were indicted for eight murders and 13 shootings in 1994. The mayhem was the result of a turf war over a neighborhood drug business that earned $5 million a year. An enforcer for the gang was said to employ a semiautomatic pistol with a laser-beam sighting attachment. To terrorize residents and competitors, he would point the red laser beam at their chest to dramatize his power to kill them by simply squeezing the trigger.[17]

Also in New York City, within three months of the above incident, two other drug gangs were rounded up by the police. One of the gangs, La Compania, employed as many as 150 people working two 12-hour shifts, processing, packaging and selling cocaine to the tune of more than $1 million a week. The indictment named 64 gang members, and included a triple murder that occurred during a shootout with a rival drug gang that had invaded their territory. An enforcer from La Compania was also killed in the gun battle, and an innocent bystander was wounded.[18] The other gang, known as the Young City Boys, was charged with selling $350,000 per week worth of crack cocaine. Thirty-three alleged members of that gang faced both murder and drug charges.[19]

Police arrested 10 members of a drug-selling gang in Liberty City, Florida, known as the Boulder Boys, on an indictment charging them with selling crack cocaine, operating a continuing criminal enterprise, and killing two people. Both of the dead were said to be innocent bystanders killed when gang members were trying to retaliate for the robbery of one of their drug-storage locations, or stash houses. In one case, they fired an assault rifle indiscriminately into the interior of a house where they thought their rival was staying. He was not there, but Althea Barron, who neither knew the intended victim nor was connected in any way with the incident, died in a hail of bullets. The other innocent party was shot to death because he just happened to be sitting in the car of the intended victim at the wrong time. According to the indictment, the gang never got the man it was after.[20]

This kind of random violence, characterized by a total lack of regard for human life, is a result of the violent and amoral character of those attracted to the illegal-drug business. With our present drug policies, we reward vicious behavior with grotesquely inflated profits. Even robbing banks presents more risk and fewer opportunities. Nearly everyone despises a bank robber, but far from being vilified, drug dealers are seen by many as simply supplying what the populace wants.

High prices as much as drug cravings push individuals toward drug-related crime. "Donovan," a 47-year-old heroin addict from Los Angeles, admitted to a reporter in 1993 that he committed 15 to 20 crimes each week to feed his habit. By stealing equipment from parked cars and shoplifting, with an occasional burglary, Donovan had $4,000 to $5,000 worth of merchandise per week to sell for about 10 cents on the dollar. His net was $400 to $500 per week.[21] If heroin were legal he could support his habit for less than $10 per week under any legalized pricing paradigm.

The centerpiece of our present drug policy, prohibition, builds on the flawed premise that if we pass laws prohibiting the possession and use of a commodity desired by a substantial percentage of our citizens, people will stop demanding it. But drugs have not disappeared, and one unintended consequence of the prohibition policy has been the development of a robust black market. The tremendous profits are then used to further subvert society, as users, strapped to pay for their expensive drugs, become dealers and recruit friends and associates into drug use. Some lawless users steal to be able to pay the inflated black-market price for their drug of choice. Lure of easy money from drug dealing subverts public officials, as cash-rich drug dealers use part of their profits to bribe public officials of both the United States and its neighbors. Violence results from the inevitable conflicts of a profitable, illegal marketplace. These pathologies are bought and paid for by the seemingly unlimited flow of illegal drug profits. People of goodwill can disagree about the pros and cons of legalizing drugs. However, there can be no real debate over drug-related violence. With legalization it would virtually disappear. Shootouts between rival drug gangs, killings for the sake of intimidation, robbery by one lawless drug dealer of another — all these acts of drug-related violence would no longer have a motive.

# 5

---

# CIVIL LIBERTIES: THE WAR WITHIN THE WAR ON DRUGS

*I will use treatment to help the sick according to my ability and judgment but never with a view of injury or wrong-doing.*

HIPPOCRATES

*. . . war is politics carried out with bloodshed.*

MAO ZEDONG

How much better off America would be if it had chosen to address the drug problem with the healing wisdom of Hippocrates rather than the punitive metaphor of war. In the name of "winning the war on drugs," the United States has allowed expediency to trump constitutional principle. Rather than trying to heal the unwell, we have caused the reordering of many of the precious priorities we call civil liberties. We have traded treatment centers for the overcrowded colleges of crime we call prisons. The right to a prompt and fair trial has been squandered, for inundated courts simply cannot mete out the quality of justice to which we are entitled. Due process has been bargained away in favor of warrantless searches and unconstitutional seizures of property, all to demonstrate "zero tolerance." As surely as the drug abuser made a wrong choice and ended up in trouble, we, as a nation, have made the wrong choice in our approach to the drug problem. We should be preventing, not punishing. The need is for education, not incarceration, treatment, not torment.

## Is Government Our Master or Our Servant?

When government intervenes where it has neither a rightful place nor any competence — that is, in trying to regulate personal choice — it fails. Thomas Jefferson observed, "Was the government to prescribe to us our medicine and diet, our bodies would be in such keeping as our souls are now. Thus, in France the emetic was once forbidden as a medicine, the potato as an article of food."

Few would agree that government has a right to tell a citizen what to read. Certainly, there are harmful books just as there are harmful substances. How about what we eat? It is arguable that more physical harm ensues from eating food high in cholesterol than from smoking marijuana. No one has ever died from the physiological effects of smoking marijuana, while tens of thousands of people die each year from heart disease, a direct result of a high-cholesterol diet. Are we to follow France's one-time example and outlaw certain foods?

If government has any role in the control of our minds and bodies, it should be as a lighthouse warning us of dangers. It's true that we need to be reminded of the perils of excessive salt, high-fat diets, and dangerous drugs. If we choose to ignore the warnings and risk the rocks and shoals of intemperance, as many of us will, that is a matter of individual choice. Government has neither the right nor the duty to punish us for our foolishness. Individual responsibility is the very essence of personal liberty.

## Those Who Agree on Little Else, Agree on This

It would be difficult to find another subject on which the American Civil Liberties Union (ACLU), William F. Buckley, Jr., former Secretary of State George P. Shultz, Senator Daniel Patrick Moynihan and the economist Milton Friedman all agree. Their common ground is that the war on drugs is destructive of our civil liberties. The ACLU has often taken the side of defendants caught up in the unattainable national obsession for a drug-free society, defending those harmed by drug war legislation, from indefensible prison sentences to property seizure without due process.

William Buckley, the spokesman for American conservatism, weighs in with this assessment: "It is, moreover, a duty of conservatives to give running attention to the loss of derivative liberties as a result of the general mayhem caused by traffic in illegal drugs, even as it was a duty, and still is, to acknowledge the implicit effects of racial discrimination on the liberty of people discriminated against."[1]

The liberal senator Daniel Patrick Moynihan takes the measure of the effects of the drug war on our civil liberties when he observes: "It is essential that we understand that by choosing [drug] prohibition we are choosing to have an intense crime problem concentrated among minorities. . . . Clearly, federal drug policy is responsible for a degree of social regression for which there does not appear to be any equivalent in our history."[2]

Former secretary of state George Shultz is one of the authors and original signers of a resolution circulated by a group of respected leaders who question the value of the war on drugs. The purpose of the resolution was to ask Congress to study the problem and come up with a more enlightened approach. No such study has been initiated, but the substance of the resolution provides a clear definition of the problem:

*Whereas, the overall situation regarding the use of drugs in our society and the crime and misery that accompany it has continued to deteriorate for several decades; and*

*Whereas, our society has continued to attempt, at enormous financial cost and loss of civil liberties, to resolve drug problems through the criminal justice system, with the accompanying increases of prisons and numbers of inmates; and*

*Whereas, the huge untaxed revenues generated by the illicit drug trade are undermining legitimate governments worldwide; and*

*Whereas, the present system has spawned a cycle of hostility by the incarceration of disproportionate numbers of African-Americans, Hispanics, and other minority groups; and*

*Whereas, the number of people who have contracted AIDS, hepatitis, and other diseases from contaminated hypodermic needles is epidemic under our present system; and*

*Whereas, in our society's zeal to pursue our criminal approach, legitimate medical uses for the relief of pain and suffering of patients have been suppressed.*

*Therefore be it resolved that our society must recognize drug use and abuse as the medical and social problems that they are and that they must be treated with medical and social solutions.*

Milton Friedman, the Nobel Prize–winning economist and one of the authors of the resolution, wrote to William Bennett, drug czar in the Reagan administration, to admonish him about his hawkish stance in the drug war:

*The path you propose of more police, more jails, . . . harsh penalties for drug users, and a whole panoply of repressive measures can only make a bad situation worse. The drug war cannot be won by those tactics without undermining the human liberty and individual freedom that you and I cherish. . . .*

*Your mistake is in failing to recognize that the very measures you favor are a major source of the evils you deplore. . . .*

*Drugs are a tragedy for addicts. But criminalizing their use converts that tragedy into a disaster for society, for users and non-users alike. Our experience with the prohibition of drugs is a replay of our experience with the prohibition of alcoholic beverages.*[3]

## The Frustration/Repression Cycle

Misdirected public policy, especially when clad in the armor of good intentions, carries with it the very real threat of repression. For example, drug-war initiatives, even though begun with the best of motives, fail because their objective of a drug-free America is unattainable. But because of the unassailable motives of the initiators, they can justify ever more desperate measures. The tight spiral of initiation, failure, and more desperate measures can result in a creeping loss of civil liberties.

Examples are legion. A bill was introduced in Congress in 1982 to establish an arctic gulag for convicted drug offenders. A Republican task force actually proposed the confiscation of 25 percent of the adjusted gross income *and* net assets of anyone caught merely possessing an illegal substance. A proposal was made to shoot down any aircraft crossing our borders that had not filed a flight plan. Although these ideas were rejected,[4] that they were introduced in a powerful deliberative body, the Congress of the United States, illustrates the potential for excess inherent in our drug policy.

Less theoretical, and even more sobering, are the many examples of policies actually put in place as a result of drug war hysteria.

A strong connection exists between gang activity and drug selling, as some gangs finance their operations and define their turf, based on drug sales. This nexus between gang activity in general and drug selling in particular makes gangs an inviting target for local law enforcement. The greater Los Angeles area is perhaps the nation's most gang-infested region. It is also home to some of the most constitutionally questionable tactics employed by local law enforcement to combat gangs.

Faced with rampant gang-related drug selling in their neighborhood, a group of concerned citizens in Panorama City, California, a suburb of Los Angeles, got a preliminary injunction in 1993 making it unlawful to possess, within a certain area of the city, a pager, a cellular telephone, or a glass bottle, all items frequently used in the drug trade but also used by people for legitimate purposes.[5] Other cities in the area obtained similar injunctions. Predictably, along with some arrests and convictions, long, expensive, and uncertain appeals have absorbed much judicial time and talent.

For the laudable purpose of cutting down heavy drug dealing in a particular neighborhood of North Hills, another Los Angeles suburb, police set up permanent roadblocks requiring a police-issued resident's permit to get through. At first applauding and financing the barriers, residents asked, some three and a half years later, that they be removed. The barriers were no longer effective and had contributed to the area's isolation and a general decline in property values.[6]

In 1992, police in Lawrence, Massachusetts, set up barriers to some troubled neighborhoods there, for much the same reason as in North Hills — with similar results. They added a different wrinkle by sending letters to the registered owners of nonresident vehicles passing through the checkpoints warning that their vehicles had been seen in a drug- and crime-infested area. Jerome Skolnick, a law professor at the University of California–Berkeley who has authored several books about police techniques, said, "There's something tasteless about this whole business. . . . It's a form of harassment that, legally, is right on the borderline."[7]

Ohio employed another highly questionable technique in its war on drugs. During one 10-month period, highway patrolmen stopped 1,339 motorists for traffic violations and requested permission to search their vehicles. According to Sgt. John Born, patrol spokesman, more than 90 percent of the motorists consented to the search, and about one in six searches produced drugs. Born said, "We're out there making traffic arrests anyhow; we go just a step further and get people transporting drugs."[8] That "just a step further" has profound constitutional implications. The policy had some short-term benefits, but many would question the long-term effect on civil liberties of searches without probable cause. What about the civil liberties of the five out of six motorists who had no drugs? Their "consent" is a dubious argument. It would take uncommon courage for a motorist, quaking from a patrol car's flashing lights, to refuse a request to search.

Police in Broward County, Florida, used an even more efficient method of waging the drug war, to the consternation of the Florida Supreme Court. As a result of mass searches of intercity buses passing through their jurisdiction, Broward police arrested Terrence Bostick after finding cocaine in his traveling bag. He denied that he had consented to a search. After reviewing the case on appeal, the court declared: "Roving patrols, random sweeps and arbitrary searches would go far to eliminate [drug courier] crime in this state. Nazi Germany, Soviet Russia, and Communist Cuba have demonstrated all too tellingly the effectiveness of such methods. Yet we are not a state that subscribes to the notion that ends justify means."[9]

The prize for the silliest antidrug law goes to Alexandria, Virginia, where you will be sent to prison for up to two years for loitering 15 minutes and "hav[ing] at least two face-to-face contacts with others that last for less than two minutes, and involve motions consistent with an exchange of money or other small objects." The ACLU, predictably offended by the law, argued convincingly that the ordinance could justify the arrest of a lawyer handing out his or his clients' business cards.[10]

Many cities tried to get rid of public telephones, the favorite communication tool of drug buyers and sellers, hoping to do serious harm to the drug trade. In these days of the beeper, the pager, and pocket-sized cellular telephones, the premise is laughable. The humor, however, is lost on the thousands of low-income families in Chicago who once depended on public telephones for both basic and emergency communication. In 1994, at Mayor Richard Daley's urging, 500 public phones were pulled from outside liquor stores and taverns and from residential streets. He originally wanted to yank

15,000 of the offending instruments, but was forced to compromise with angry telephone executives and users. Said the mayor: "People are outraged. They see drug dealers using those phones twenty-four hours a day, seven days a week in front of their homes."[11] He did not divulge how the people differentiated between drug dealers and innocent callers.

## Big Brother Is Watching Even in the Doctor's Office

The national mania to cleanse our society of drugs has intruded into the doctor's office. Apart from the issue of privacy, but no less important is the humane imperative that a person suffer no more pain than is necessary in a medical situation. Pain treatment among cancer patients, many of them terminal, has been compromised by the intrusion of federal and state drug officials. Frank Adams, an Arlington, Texas, pain specialist, chafes under the pressure of 18 searches by DEA and local police checking his patient files. He has stated: "Drug agents have been turned loose and are totally out of control, and they do not know how to discriminate between the legitimate and illegitimate use of these drugs. This is police-state medicine!"[12]

The Agency for Health Care Policy and Research says, "Perhaps the most persistent barrier to effective pain control is the unfounded belief that using such drugs will result in addiction."[13] Other experts in pain management explain that doctors often misread a patient's asking for drugs as a sign of addiction and withhold the drugs, resulting in undertreatment for the pain.[14]

## The Medical Use of Marijuana

To deny patients painkilling medication that is consistent with sound medical practice is to deny them their full measure of civil liberties. Too often, the use of opiates is withheld based on drug war-inspired fears, which often results in inhumane under-medication for pain.

Ingesting marijuana, either by smoking or eating, has been shown to provide dramatic relief from the nausea of cancer chemotherapy. A Harvard University study of doctors' attitudes concerning the medical use of marijuana revealed that 40 percent of participating cancer specialists recommended that their patients undergoing chemotherapy use marijuana. Nearly half (48 percent) said they would prescribe it if it were legal.[15] With only an eight percent spread between the number of doctors who recommended marijuana and those who would if it were legal, a clear indication for the medical use of marijuana exists.

Medical benefits of marijuana go well beyond cancer patients. AIDS sufferers are beset with nausea from AZT, Interferon, and other drugs. The wasting syndrome, often present in the later stages of AIDS, is relieved by marijuana, bringing about dramatic improvements in the patient's appetite. Glaucoma sufferers relieve pressure within the eyeball by ingesting marijuana. Relaxing the stiff muscles of those who suffer from spastic paralysis and multiple sclerosis is another humane use of the drug. Indeed, the therapeutic value of marijuana has been endorsed by the 48,000-member American Medical Student Association.[16]

A combination of political posturing and misguided policy has conspired to deny patients marijuana relief. As early as 1978, a federal program allowed sufferers of painful, sometimes terminal, illnesses to apply for the legal use of marijuana. The Bush administration terminated the program, contending that the dangers in the use of the drug might outweigh its benefits. At that time 15 people were receiving medical marijuana from the government.[17] Only one new application has since been approved. Various sources report that seven to ten of the original group are still alive and obtaining the drug legally from the government, but thousands of other patients have either become criminals by purchasing marijuana through the black market or still suffer in silence.

In 1971 Harvard psychiatry professor Lester Grinspoon finally decided to assume the risk of obtaining medical marijuana for his dying son. Starting in 1967, before his son fell ill or had any contact with marijuana, the professor had conducted research on marijuana, hoping to prove to young people that they were taking a dangerous drug. Four years later, when his son was diagnosed as having leukemia and began chemotherapy, which caused debilitating nausea, the professor refused to have his son use marijuana because it was illegal. But Grinspoon's wife, driven by a mother's despair, had the boy try some of the illegal weed just before a chemotherapy session. The results were dramatic: Instead of the usual hours of vomiting after the day's session, the young man asked for something to eat. Although his son died, Professor Grinspoon went on to coauthor a book entitled *Marijuana: The Forbidden Medicine.* He said he had been "brainwashed" about marijuana and commented, "When this country comes to its senses, it will see it as a miracle medicine, a remarkably versatile substance with very limited toxicity. If you scour the medical literature, you cannot find a death due to [marijuana] ."[18]

A 79-year-old Monticello, New York, grandmother, Mildred Kaitz, was arrested for growing marijuana. No latter-day "Ma Barker," she was growing it for her son who suffered from multiple sclerosis. This degenerative disease of the nervous system had left him with crippled legs, blurred vision, and no appetite. After learning that a marijuana cigarette had stimulated his appetite, she set out to buy him an illegal supply. She was shocked to find that $50 bought an amount no bigger than a packet of sugar. "My God," she said, "fifty dollars! I'll grow it for my son."[19] And she did. Growing her own plants, harvesting the buds, and drying them in her basement, she filled a gallon jar, from which she would send her son a periodic ration. When neighbors asked what her strange-looking plants were, she answered, "Marijuana." Most thought she was just joking, but word eventually got back to the local police and she was arrested. A kindly village judge understood the situation and put Kaitz on probation. But her son now has to do without his maternal stash, as he hopes for the day when government regulations will no longer stand between him and relief from his relentless symptoms.

When that day finally comes, it will be due in no small way to people like the Grinspoons, Mrs. Kaitz, and Kenny and Barbara Jenks, a Florida couple who contracted AIDS as a result of tainted blood used to treat Kenny's hemophilia.[20] From a friend the couple learned that marijuana would help stimulate their appetites lost through the effects of AZT and other nausea-producing drugs. Barbara was near death from malnutrition when they smoked their first joint. It worked wonders on her appetite and Kenny's as well. When they began growing their own marijuana plants, they were promptly arrested. After an agonizing nine-month legal battle, the couple was allowed to buy marijuana from the federal government, the only new application approved since the Bush administration ordered a stop to the program. Barbara lived for two more springs. She preceded Kenny in death, but not before their arrest was expunged from the record — one of Barbara's last wishes. The couple's widely reported efforts to secure justice left a legacy of grit and determination among those battling for medical marijuana.

In spite of hundreds of cases where patients have been helped by marijuana, the U.S. government persists in the position that more research is needed to determine the scientific efficacy of marijuana. However, no administration has yet been willing to fund and authorize the necessary research. Herein lies the irony: Government officials know the law prohibiting the medical use of marijuana is questionable, but are unwilling to risk the political heat of continuing research.

The impasse over the medical use of marijuana was finally broken by the initiative process in California and Arizona in 1996, as both states approved measures to legalize the sale of marijuana for medical purposes. As of 1997, six other states also had medical marijuana laws, and such laws were pending in five more, plus Washington, D.C.[21] Conflicts between state and federal law complicate implementation.

## The Tenth Amendment

The tenth amendment to the U.S. Constitution reserves to the states those powers not delegated to the federal government. In one of the more blatant breaches of this provision, Congress in 1992 approved legislation *requiring* the states to pass a law suspending for six months the driver's license of anyone convicted of a drug infraction, no matter how minor. Congress gave the states the choice of either passing such a law or passing a resolution explicitly rejecting the proposition (and thus appearing to their electorates to be soft on drugs). If they did neither, the states would risk not receiving their share of federal highway funds.

California's governor, Pete Wilson, demonstrated his dedication as a drug warrior by vetoing the legislature's attempt to opt out of such a harsh penalty. Two years later, under the threat of losing millions of federal highway dollars, the legislature passed and Wilson signed a bill providing for the mandated driver's-license suspension. It was estimated that in the first year of enforcement, 131,000 California drivers would lose their licenses as a result. Evan Nossoff, a spokesman for the California Department of Motor Vehicles, said, "Mainly, we looked at the impact of losing between $47 and $55 million."[15] The good news is that 31 states had the fortitude not to blink in this game of legislative chicken.[23] The bad news is that the U.S. Congress would pass so constitutionally intrusive a bill in the first place.

## Mushrooms Versus the Scales of Justice

A case involving psychedelic mushrooms illustrates the intricate dance of our courts to preserve civil liberties while waging war on drugs. In 1990, an Oneonta, New York, college student was arrested with two pounds of illegal mushrooms. These fungi grow wild, and certain species are prized for their hallucinogenic qualities. Only after the fungi's popularity brought them into conflict with the prohibitionist objectives of the drug war were they listed as controlled substances. At issue in the student's case was the question of how much of the active hallucinogen, psilocybin, there was in the two-pound cache of fungus. Neither the student nor the police chemist who testified at his trial had the least notion of how much psilocybin resided in the two pounds of mushrooms. Nonetheless, it is a felony in California to possess 625 milligrams (slightly less than the amount of aspirin in two typical tablets) or more of the hallucinogen. Below that amount, possession is a misdemeanor. Mushroom users, or "schroomers," know that mushrooms vary greatly in their hallucinogenic qualities. Most species, in fact, have none. The hapless student, originally found guilty of possessing a felonious amount of psilocybin and, because it was his second felony, sentenced to ten years to life in prison, subsequently had his felony conviction overturned on appeal because he did not "knowingly" possess the felonious amount of psilocybin.

Terrence Conner, the chairman of the New York State Bar Association's Criminal Justice Division, agreed with the California reversal: "Where penalties are enhanced by the weight of the product, the prosecution should have to prove that element of the crime."[24]

## When Does a Tax Become a Fine?

In response to the rising pitch of drug war hysteria during the 1980s and early 1990s, no less than 28 states passed laws to tax those in possession of illegal drugs, a ludicrous idea that does violence to both the principle of fair taxation and respect for the rule of law. On the one hand, the government asserts it is illegal to possess marijuana and cocaine; on the other, it then demands payment of a tax for possession. In a two-to-one decision, the Third District Court of Appeals, ruling on a Florida case, held that if a person is compelled by a law to report the ownership of an illegal drug on a tax return, that law violates the citizen's constitutional right against self-incrimination.[25]

In a similarly close five-to-four decision, the United States Supreme Court held that if a person is forced to pay a tax after being convicted of possession of a controlled substance, that "tax" is really a fine and amounts to double jeopardy.[26] All laws against possession already carry stiff fines and other sanctions. Furthermore, taxes are typically levied and collected by the administrative branch of government, not the judicial branch, whose business is to assess fines and ensure their collection.

The Supreme Court case centered on Montana rancher Richard Kurth and his family's conviction for growing marijuana. The rancher and his wife did not appeal their convictions and served prison sentences. Three of their adult children and two of their spouses received suspended sentences. They lost their 4,500-acre family ranch to bankruptcy. Then Kurth was presented with a tax bill for $848,000, under Montana's Dangerous Drug Tax Act.[27] The bill was later reduced by a bankruptcy judge to $181,000. The original tax was based on the amount of marijuana seized and was equal to 3 to 16 times its street value (depending on quality and where it was sold).[28] So high a tax, in relation to the value of the commodity, makes clear that this was a fine and not a tax.

The narrow decision to overturn the law saw Justices Souter, Blackmun, Kennedy, and Ginsburg join Justice Stevens in the majority opinion. Agreeing with Chief Justice Rehnquist in dissent were Justices O'Connor, Scalia, and Thomas. Justice Souter wondered if the amount of the tax would increase "every time a marijuana plant comes up with a few new shoots." Chief Justice Rehnquist did not consider the tax to be so high "as to be deemed arbitrary or shocking." Justice Stevens, in a masterpiece of understatement, observed, "It's a little bit unusual to tax something that a person is not permitted to own." On a somewhat more forceful tack, he pointed out the absurdity of the law by asking whether people would be allowed to keep their drugs as long as they paid their taxes.[29]

Despite that decision, many states with these tax laws on their books still circumvent the spirit of the court's decision. North Carolina is the top drug-tax collector among the 28 states with such laws. It has collected ten times more revenue than any other state from this source, some $26,000,000, violating the constitutional rights of at least 20,000 North Carolinians. Not coincidentally, police and sheriff's departments get 75 percent of the take.[30]

Instead of being guided toward more constitutional behavior by the Supreme Court's decision, some states keep right on taxing drug defendants. Never mind civil liberties. This is war.

## The Tyranny of Asset Forfeiture

A far more widely used drug war weapon, one with fallout even more deadly to our civil liberties, is asset forfeiture. This body of law enables law enforcement agencies — federal, state, or local — to seize any assets either used in a drug transaction or acquired with money made through selling drugs. These sound like reasonable, even laudable, objectives. The problems arise, as they do in so much of the war on drugs, when people overzealously pursue objectives imbued with the urgency of war. Likewise, when money can be had as a by-product of doing in the enemy, the combination becomes irresistible.

Before examining the many problems of our present forfeiture laws, it is well to understand their history, which goes back to the 1700s and to English common law, on which our legal system is based. Those early statutes provided for the seizure of ships whose owners failed to pay customs duties on their ship cargoes. Such duties were a vital source of revenue in the early days of our republic; consequently, the first U.S. Congress enacted forfeiture laws as a civil sanction for nonpayment.

A legal fiction exists in civil law to this day that the asset — the ship, the house, or the ill-gotten goods being seized — committed the crime and not the owner. This gives rise to some interesting seizure cases, such as *United States vs. James Daniel Good Real Property* and *United States vs. 667 Bottles of Wine.* The operation of the seizure statutes under civil, rather than criminal, law enables the law enforcement agency simply to show, as grounds for the seizure, "probable cause" that the asset was used in, or acquired through, drug activity, a much lower standard than "beyond reasonable doubt," the requirement for criminal cases. Furthermore, in civil cases, the asset can be taken without ever convicting its owner of a crime or, indeed, even charging him with one. Congressman Henry Hyde of Illinois stated in 1993 that 80 percent of the people whose property is seized by the federal government under drug laws are never charged with a crime.[31]

When luxury cars, yachts, airplanes, and homes, not to mention huge quantities of cash belonging to drug dealers, are hunting grounds for drug warriors and require only a simple search warrant, abuses are inevitable.

Four years after their son pleaded guilty to growing marijuana in their backyard for his own use, Mr. and Mrs. Joseph Lopes of Maui, Hawaii, were informed by the local police that their house would be seized because of their son's earlier transgression. A Maui detective who was nosing around for missed forfeiture opportunities discovered the case and recognized that the law allowed him to seize the parents' property because they knew of their son's crime. While seizures were uncommon at that time, agencies have learned how to use the law and have seen the financial payoff, according to Assistant U.S. Attorney Marshall Silverberg of Honolulu.[32]

Headed home from a family reunion, the Grady McClendon family, complete with grandchildren, made a wrong turn in Fitzgerald, Georgia, in more ways than one. Police stopped them for the minor traffic violation and asked for permission to search their car. The search revealed jewelry, $2,300 in cash, a registered handgun, and ten lottery tickets, along with a stick of what the police said was cocaine. After being detained for six hours, the family was released, but not until the police had seized the cash and some other belongings as drug paraphernalia. Upon later examination, the stick of cocaine turned out to be bubble gum. Eleven months later, a judge ordered the McClendons' belongings returned. The prosecutor in the case, James E. Turk, was unrepentant. He characterized the incident as ". . . a good stop. They had no proof of where they lived beyond drivers' licenses. They had jewelry that could have been contraband . . . and they had more cash than I would expect them to carry." If that, plus bubble gum, constitute probable cause, properly-tied gum chewers beware!

## Mixing Money and Law Enforcement

Adding the power of greed to the function of law enforcement is an exciting idea to many in a nation that owes most of its prosperity to the entrepreneurial spirit. Cambridge, Massachusetts, police sergeant John K. Jones proclaimed, "Seizing assets lets everyone know that if you want to deal drugs and drive fancy cars, we'll take them away from you."[33] What he didn't say is that these spoils have purchased, or otherwise provided, vehicles, new semiautomatic weapons, computers and other tools of police work for his department. Fair enough, until other local agencies come along demanding a piece of the action. Given all the substantive problems with which local government must contend, do we really need agencies squabbling about who gets what from the latest drug bust? Declared The *Boston Globe*, "The issue threatens to turn into a full-blown fight in cities like Cambridge as police departments rely more and more on seized assets to fund their efforts."[34] This echoes the sentiments of former New York City police commissioner Patrick Murphy, who testified to Congress, "The large monetary value of forfeitures . . . has created a great temptation for state and local police departments to target assets rather than criminal activity."[35]

In Arizona, over an 18-month period, undercover state troopers, pretending to be drug couriers, transported nearly 13 tons of marijuana from the Mexican border to drops around Tucson. They prolonged the ruse because they kept hoping to arrest the Mexican suppliers on the U.S. side of the border. Of course, the troopers knew all along that every ounce delivered was going out on their streets. The rationale? Along with 20 arrests, the sting netted $3,000,000 for the state forfeiture fund.

Lest anyone dismiss the forfeiture problem as local or insignificant, it should be noted that the DEA alone seized over $645 million in assets in 1995.[36] No figures are published for the combined asset seizures of the 50 states, but over 90 percent of drug arrests are made by state and local law enforcement agencies. The Feds have utilized asset seizure in over 200,000 cases since 1985, netting participating state and local law enforcement agencies over $1 billion.[37] While this has helped local government budgets, it comes at too high a price in confidence. Respect for the law is too precious to be endangered by questionable motives. Profit seeking serves us well in the arenas of business and economics, but has no place in law enforcement.

Asset seizure also has racial overtones. Law enforcement people often use "profiles" to help them target their efforts more efficiently. Because of the disproportionate participation of African Americans in the drug trade, they are sometimes singled out based on nothing more than the color of their skin. The DEA maintains confiscation squads at most major city airports; they pay a 10 percent bounty to ticket agents and others who spot people paying cash for tickets or displaying other characteristics frequently seen in drug dealers. In 1992, *60 Minutes* aired a segment in which a well-dressed black reporter purchased airline tickets for cash in several major airports. In each case the reporter was detained by DEA agents and his cash was confiscated.[38]

## The Courts Take Notice, Finally

The abuses of asset forfeiture have not entirely escaped the notice of our higher courts, even though they have been painfully slow to react. While the value of seized assets, mostly from the drug war, increased six-fold in eight years, in 1992 a federal appeals court announced, "We continue to be enormously troubled by the government's increasing and virtually unchecked use of the civil forfeiture statues and the disregard for due process that is buried in those statutes."[39] In the same year, another federal appeals court complained that it was ". . . troubled by the government's view that any property, whether it be a hobo's hovel or the Empire State Building, can be seized by the government because the owner, regardless of his or her past criminal record, engages in a single drug transaction."[40]

Responding to that pent-up frustration within the lower courts, in *U.S. vs. A Parcel of Land*, the United States Supreme Court made three important decisions during 1993.

The first of these landmark decisions was a 6–3 ruling that the U.S. government cannot seize drug-tainted property from an owner who had no knowledge of its drug-related history. The decision was hailed by Michael Crotty of the American Bankers Association: "If the government had won, the ownership of everything in this country would have been clouded. You could never be certain you had clear title. The horror stories of forfeitures imposed on truly innocent people, years after they acquired property, should subside."[41]

In its second important drug-related decision of 1993, the court unanimously established that the Constitution limits the amount of money or property authorities may seize in drug cases. If the amount seized is unreasonable in relation to the crime, it will be considered cruel and unusual punishment. The Supreme Court left it for the lower courts to decide the formula for reasonableness. In lamenting the high court's decision, U.S. Attorney A. John Pappalardo demonstrated the flawed logic that had given rise to the tactic of seizure. "What asset forfeiture does is, it removes the incentive to engage in criminal activity in the first place. The incentive is monetary and asset forfeiture, when applied, removes the profit."[42] The truth is, asset forfeiture has had no discernible deterrent effect. Rather, it has become a form of punishment fraught with opportunities for abuse.

The third decision by the court, in 1993 (a watershed year for drug war decisions), was made in the case mentioned earlier, *United*

*States vs. James Daniel Good Real Property.* Good pleaded guilty to marijuana possession, completed his jail sentence of one year, was released on probation, and thought his case was closed. Four years later, the government seized a house he owned and began collecting rent from his tenant. There was no hearing, no litigation. After several levels of appeals, the U.S. Supreme Court ruled that both notice and a hearing are required prior to seizure, to protect the rights of the property owner.

## They're Not Shooting the Messenger;
## They're Just Ignoring Him

A medieval king was said to have ordered the death of any messenger who brought him bad news. Prosecutors in drug cases do not visit violence on those who tell them of these Supreme Court decisions; they simply ignore the message. Consequently, civil libertarians should not be overly encouraged by these three helpful decisions. Even after two of the three decisions had been handed down, Mark Sakaley, a Justice Department spokesman, opined that the decisions were not expected to have a major impact on forfeiture programs.[43] The department went so far as to issue a statement that said, in part, all along, it had "exercised restraint in enforcing civil forfeiture laws" and that "it does not expect the [ruling] to have any significant impact on the day-to-day operations of the forfeiture program."[44] Lee J. Radek, director of the Justice Department's Asset Forfeiture Office, defiantly predicted in its house organ, *Asset Forfeiture News*, that the department would come up with new methods of "innovative expansion" to get around the court's decisions.[45] The Justice Department would do well to heed the words of Justice Louis Brandeis, who declared, "The greatest dangers to liberty lurk in insidious encroachment by men of zeal, well meaning but without understanding."

# 6

━━━━◦◦◦◦◦━━━━

# CAN WE BE BOTH FREE
# AND DRUG-FREE?

## Another Time Bomb Ticks

While drug war litigation continues, the state of Michigan has come up with a new drug war strategy that could sink the nation's already overcrowded court dockets if it spreads. The law, signed by Governor John Engler in 1994, the first of its kind in the nation, provides for civil lawsuits against drug dealers in addition to the criminal charges they already face. Anyone who is mentally, physically, or fiscally affected by drugs can sue a drug dealer in a civil action under a formula that determines the presumed area of damage based on drug-sale volume. For instance, total sales of 650 grams (1.43 pounds) of cocaine, heroin, or methamphetamine would qualify the dealer to be sued by any citizen in the state. For lesser amounts sold, the plaintiff would have to live within a certain distance of the dealer within the state to have grounds for a suit.

In other words, any Michigander can say "I have been harmed by your drug selling, Mr. Dealer, and I'm going to file a civil law suit against you and your assets." Furthermore, because it is a civil rather than criminal action, the plaintiff need not prove his or her claim beyond a reasonable doubt. Nor, if the dealer has sold sufficient volume, does the plaintiff have to prove that drugs were sold in a specific area within the state or to a specific person.[1] To further attract plaintiffs, these civil suits can be filed before a criminal conviction is obtained so that substantial drug-related assets will frequently still be available. What this ill-advised legislation does is pit the public against law enforcement in competition to seize drug-related assets, an irresistible lure for litigious citizens.

The money-seeking behavior this law encourages has the potential to bury the legal system in Michigan and the four other states who had, by 1996, followed their lead.[2] Prosecutions under this law are bound to be incessantly appealed, increasing the drug war's toll on our legal system. It will not affect the behavior of drug dealers and will only result in frivolous lawsuits benefiting lawyers generously and society not at all.

## Creative Law Enforcement

The zealous drive for more and harsher drug war convictions has already resulted in some judicial nightmares. Judge Harold H. Greene, ruling in a case involving a Washington, D.C., cocaine dealer, found that the DEA agent had "unfairly manipulated" the defendant to get her to sell him crack, instead of powder cocaine, because the agent knew the sentence for crack was many times longer than the sentence for powder. He consequently reduced the dealer's sentence from 15 to 10 years. In his decision Judge Greene wrote: "The ability of a law enforcement officer to enhance a defendant's sentence through his own actions . . . shocks the conscience of the court."[3]

Some of the abuses of civil liberties occurring in the drug war stem from procedures that seem to skirt due process in the interest of more severe sentences. A particularly dangerous example, the so-called "Fatico hearing," allows prosecutors to bring up hearsay and unproven allegations about crimes of which the defendant has been accused but not convicted. A federal judge can take these accusations into consideration and sentence the defendant to a much longer sentence than judicial guidelines would specify. R. Keith Stroup, former head of the National Association of Criminal Defense Lawyers, said, "It's a quirk in the criminal justice system. They just make the allegations and you end up serving more time in prison. I think it runs counter to our whole system of justice."[4]

In another example of overzealous drug war tactics, police labs in Los Angeles and nearby Santa Ana, began cooking powdered cocaine, which they had seized, into crack to use in reverse sting operations, where police pose as drug sellers and then arrest the buyers.[5] These two law enforcement agencies evidently didn't do their homework: In Broward County, Florida, several hundred drug convictions obtained after buyers purchased police-manufactured crack from undercover officers were reversed by a state appeals court. The court felt that the police had simply gone too far.[6] Reflecting on the tactic, Bob Knox, a deputy public defender in Santa Ana, offered, "In my opinion, it's sort of an easy way to make a lot of felony arrests for drugs and show statistically that you're making busts."[7]

## Do We Really Want to Celebrate Informers?

Intelligence is a key ingredient in any war, and the drug war is no exception. Much of this intelligence is gathered by law enforcement from paid informers. According to the February 13, 1995, issue of *The National Law Journal*, federal law enforcement agencies spent $97 million on informers in 1993, up 400 percent compared to eight years earlier. Michael Levine, a 25-year veteran of the DEA and the Customs Service, criticized federal agents for "allowing about 15,000 wild, out of control informants" to take over investigations. Warned Stephen S. Trott, head of the Justice Department's Criminal Division in the Reagan administration, and now a federal appeals court judge in Boise, Idaho, "There needs to be better control and supervision of informants." Again, when money and law enforcement mix, abuses abound.

Patricia Williams, a heroin addict whose parents had died 15 years before her drug problems began and had left her a sizable estate, is serving a 10-year sentence for possession of heroin. She was tracked for 2 years by a paid informant. The informant had a written contract guaranteeing her a percentage of the assets seized as a result of Patricia's arrest. The informant's patience paid off. Among the assets seized from Patricia was a fully occupied apartment building in Manhattan that she had purchased 13 years prior to her arrest.[8]

Often, when informers are not actually paid, they relay information as part of a plea-bargaining negotiation. The motivations of money and, in some cases, less prison time often result in exaggerated or inaccurate information. Based on inaccurate information from a confidential informant, the Boston apartment of Jean-Claude and Ermite David was invaded by police. The Davids later won a $50,000 judgment from the city. A witness at the trial testified that as the officers left the Davids' apartment, one of them apologized and said, "This happens all the time."[9]

Echoing that unintended indictment, Capt. Art Binder, of the Cumberland County, North Carolina, Sheriff's Department, said, "It happens every day in this business." He spoke with some authority. His officers had recently raided two wrong houses before hitting the right one on their third try![10]

Based on bogus information from an informant whose credibility had already been called into question, DEA agents sprang a midnight raid on the home of Donald Carlson, a 41-year-old executive with no criminal record. Asleep in his home near San Diego, Carlson was awakened by the noise of his front door being battered in; thinking burglary, he came out of his bedroom armed. It is unclear who fired first, but when the shooting stopped, Carlson lay on the floor with three bullets in his body. No drugs were found. He recovered from his wounds, but suffered lasting damage to his arm, shoulder, and respiratory system. Once the U.S. government realized its error, it dropped charges, admitted liability and agreed to a $2,750,000 settlement.

A nationwide computer search by Newhouse News Service turned up 54 such botched raids in a four-year period, and according to one of its reporters, there were likely many more than that.[11] Our law enforcement agencies are the envy of most of the world. These unfortunate incidents illustrate only that our nation's all-out war on drugs has too often permitted aggressiveness to outflank reason.

One drug education program promoted rebellion among school children by encouraging them to turn in their drug-involved parents. This reverse twist on the concept of tough love resulted in a few arrests. However, such tampering with the parent-child relationship raises serious moral and ethical questions for society that far outweigh the advantage of a few arrests. Another example is a 1995 program considered seriously by the Los Angeles City Unified School District, the nation's second largest, which would have awarded a $75 gift certificate to any student who snitched on another student who bought, sold or used drugs, committed an act of vandalism, or carried a weapon to school. The adolescent informer could claim a prize by calling a hot-line number with assured confidentiality.[12] Fortunately, the program was never enacted.

## Some Drug Tests Flunk Civil Liberties

Testing urine or, with a recently developed technique, hair, for evidence of drug taking does unquestionable good in medicine and law enforcement, for doctors and nurses need to know about a patient's chemical status to minister to him intelligently. Only the most far-out civil libertarian would argue that point. Likewise, in law enforcement, society has a legitimate need to know about drug taking by arrestees, parolees, and prisoners. Yet, civil libertarians are justifiably concerned about drug testing in employee-employer contexts. Ruling on a case allowing the expansion of testing to a previously untested group of federal workers, Federal Appeals Judge Patricia Wald of Washington, D.C., wrote in her dissent that the constitutional protection against unreasonable search and seizure "is in a precarious position today ... caught in the crossfire of our nation's war on drugs."[13]

The widespread use of drug testing by employers owes its

beginning to a 1986 Reagan Presidential Commission headed by Judge Irving R. Kaufman. Its charge was to look into ways of controlling the demand for drugs. The commission hit upon the idea of requiring all federal employees and employees of companies awarded government contracts to be tested for illegal drugs. The commission also recommended that all private employers should initiate testing programs. Neither the constitutionality nor the cost seem to have been considered in this pronouncement, some of which became law.[14]

The American Management Association reported in 1997 that more of its members are testing for drugs. Its survey of major U.S. firms shows that drug tests had risen from 52 percent in 1990 to 81 percent in 1996.[15] It seems clearly intrusive of an employee's privacy to test for drug usage if no questions of the safety of others or the quality of work are involved. Equally clear seems the imperative that random testing of operators of public conveyances such as airplanes, buses, and trains is necessary and appropriate. Beyond that, the waters get murky. When appropriate, should the testing be random or en masse? Who besides the subject should be informed of a positive test result? What is the appropriate course of action following a positive test, treatment or termination? How does an employer handle the conundrum that casual users neither need nor will benefit from treatment, while addicted users might, and tests cannot differentiate between the two?

Adding to the murk is the question of the efficacy of testing as a drug-use preventive. A 20-member panel, whose study was funded by The National Institute on Drug Abuse, took an exhaustive look at the question, and concluded there was little scientific evidence that workplace drug testing had any effect on drug usage. Bradford Googins, an associate professor at the Boston University School of Social Work and a member of the panel, stated, "This is a huge business, this drug testing, and you have to prove to me it's worth all this expense and energy. The proof is not there as far as I can see." Dr. Charles P. O'Brien, director of the study, worried about the inconsistency between the concern of employers about drinking as compared to their concern about drugs. He imagined a scenario where a manager "just returned from a two-martini lunch and actually under the influence" would have to confront a subordinate who tested positive for marijuana used several days ago, but not at work.[16]

## Mandatory Minimum Sentences: More Damage to Civil Liberties

The Sentencing Guidelines, authorized by Congress as part of the 1984 Comprehensive Crime Control Act and the 1986 federal Mandatory Minimum Sentences System both affect a judge's discretion in sentencing convicted drug criminals.

The sentencing guidelines established procedures to assist federal judges to maintain consistency in sentences from one court to the other. Armed robbery by a first-time offender with a certain amount of money involved and no bodily harm to the victim should result in the same sentence in Oklahoma as it does in Ohio, a commonsense proposition generally supported by the nation's judges. By 1993, the guidelines had been amended some 500 times but were still widely considered to help formulate more consistent and rational sentences. Guidelines can be exceeded or reduced with written justification by the judge. More than half the states have established similar procedures for state courts, and more will follow.

The story of mandatory minimum sentences is not so positive. In the ebb and flow of the war on drugs, when a surge of drug use, real or imagined, occurs, a cry goes up for a "solution." Political leaders responding to pressure from their constituents churn out more public policy to stamp out the scourge of drugs. But because these policies have an impossible objective — to eliminate illicit drug use — they are doomed to failure. Yet 46 states had passed some kind of mandatory minimum sentencing law by 1993.

When Nelson Rockefeller was governor of New York, heroin was the problem drug of the day. In 1973, in his zeal to clamp down on its burgeoning use in New York, the governor ramrodded legislation known as the Rockefeller Laws through the state legislature in Albany. A study of the efficacy of the Rockefeller Laws was commissioned by the Association of the Bar of the City of New York in 1976. It found "no evidence of a sustained reduction in heroin use after 1973" and noted that "the pattern of stable heroin use in New York City between 1973 and mid-1976 was not appreciably different from the average pattern in other East Coast cities."[17]

The central weakness of mandatory minimum sentences is that they substitute rigid rules for the judgment of judge and jury. Lawrence V. Cipollone, Jr., now serving 15 years to life in New York's Downstate Correctional Facility, was arrested for selling 2.34 ounces of cocaine to an undercover officer. He points out that "Amy Fisher will be out in four years and ten months for shooting that woman in the head, and Robert Chambers got five years for the Central Park strangling." If Mr. Cipollone had been in possession of .35 of an ounce less, his sentence under the mandatory sentencing laws would have been three years.[18] This misguided legislation also leads to the substitution by drug dealers of juveniles too young to come under the jurisdiction of the sentencing laws as carriers and sellers of drugs. So large a number of arrests of minors in New York occurred that police had to quit arresting them for this offense temporarily, because the juvenile division of the criminal justice system was unable to handle the caseload.[19]

Grotesque inconsistencies also result. Under federal law, possession of either 100 marijuana plants or 100 grams of heroin carry identical mandatory minimum sentences of 5 to 40 years without parole. In America's prisons today, there are more than 30 people serving life sentences for the crime of growing marijuana. Contrast that with an American convicted of murder who spends, on average, less than nine years in prison.[20]

Federal Judge Alan H. Nevas of Connecticut became enormously frustrated when mandatory minimum sentencing usurped his judicial prerogatives in the case of a 20-year-old first-time offender, Keith Edwards. The transcript of the sentencing hearing reveals his outrage:

*I have been sitting now as a judge for almost seven years. And in my view, I think the sentence which I am being forced to impose on you is one of the unfairest sentences that I have ever had to impose. Now, I don't excuse your conduct, obviously. You knew what you were doing. You were out there selling crack. You were making money, and you deserve to be punished, and you deserve to go to jail. But ten years at your age is just absolutely outrageous, as far as I'm concerned. And I resent the fact that the Congress has forced me, and put me in a position where I have to send a young man like you to jail for ten years for a crime that doesn't deserve more than three or four.*

In a similar situation, Judge J. Spencer Letts of the Central District of California was faced with a case involving 27-year-old Johnny Patillo, who had no prior criminal record, a college education and a steady job. Temporarily financially strapped, Patillo succumbed to the temptation of making a fast $500 by mailing a package, which he admitted knowing contained drugs, for a neighbor. Patillo, a basic drug "mule," was unaware of the amount or type of drug in the package: Both of these factors determined the calculation of his mandatory sentence. For his indiscretion Patillo received the mandatory minimum sentence of 10 years in prison. Like Judge Nevas in Connecticut, Judge Letts expressed his outrage:

*The minimum ten-year sentence to be served by defendant was determined by Congress before he ever committed a criminal act. Congress decided to hit the problem of drugs with a sledgehammer, making no allowance for the circumstances of any particular case. Under this sledgehammer approach, it can make no difference whether defendant actually owned the drugs with which he was caught. . . . It can make no difference whether he is a lifetime criminal or a first-time offender. Indeed, under this sledgehammer approach, it could make no difference if the day before making this one slip in an otherwise unblemished life, defendant had rescued 15 children from a burning building, or had won the Congressional Medal of Honor while defending his country."*[21]

Twenty-plus years have shown that although mandatory minimum sentencing may have been well intentioned, it's also ineffective, unfair, and an insult to civil liberties. Arrests for drug law violations since the 1986 date of the federal mandatory minimum sentencing law have increased from 824,000 to over 1,500,000 in 1996.[22] As a result, not only has a great hue and cry gone up from civil libertarians but the judicial establishment itself has emphatically said, "Enough!" The most effective statement by the judiciary came from a group of 50 of the 680 senior federal judges who announced, to the consternation of many politicians and other drug warriors, that they would no longer take drug cases because of the wrongs done by mandatory sentencing laws. This was immediately met by demands from some politicians that the judges either recant or resign. With judicial aplomb, they pointed out that as senior judges they were guided by "United States Code, Title 28, Section 294 (b), which states that a senior judge may perform such judicial duties as he is willing and able to undertake."[23] In spite of this and other opposition, mandatory minimum drug sentences continue to exist.

## Neighborhoods Become Battlegrounds

Because of the disproportionate involvement in drugs of those on the lower end of the socioeconomic scale, poor neighborhoods suffer the most in the war on drugs. In efforts to "clean up" neighborhoods, police have trampled on the civil liberties of many citizens. In Birmingham, Alabama, whenever a drug arrest takes place in a rental property, police write a letter informing the landlord of the arrest. If, after the second arrest of the same tenant, the landlord has not initiated eviction proceedings against the tenant, law enforcement agents can themselves evict the tenant. Interviews with two different property management firms that together manage over 2,200 units in and around Birmingham revealed strong support of a program some consider an invasion of the rights to due process of the evicted tenants. No convictions are necessary for eviction, only two arrests.

Throughout California, community activists have copied a strategy originally developed in the northern city of Oakland whereby residents who feel aggrieved or threatened by drug activity in a landlord's building can sue the landlord in small claims court. Cases come up within 30 days instead of the months or years associated with conventional litigation, and the $5,000 small claims maximum can be multiplied several times over simply by several neighbors suing the same landlord at once in separate complaints.[24]

In Quincy, Massachusetts, Donna Spenser, an admitted drug user, was evicted from her apartment at the Willard Street housing complex because she had been charged with possession of cocaine, charged but not convicted. Indeed, the case had not come to trial when she was evicted. Police in Quincy explained that they were trying to clean up drug-blighted areas. In the words of Police Chief Francis E. Mullen, "The way we look at it, we're out to help the neighborhood."[25] As part of a nationwide program, the DEA has trained officers in Quincy and in more than 400 other police departments throughout New England how to obtain drug-related evictions from rental housing.

From the Chicago Housing Authority, which runs public housing in that city, come the words of Kristin Anderson, their spokesperson: "Our standard [for eviction] in a civil proceeding is that the resident is involved in a criminal matter, not convicted."[26] The act of eviction prior to conviction reveals an assumption of guilt rather than the presumption of innocence that is the cornerstone of the

American justice system. And the drug dealing does not cease; it merely moves to another neighborhood.

## Unreasonable Search and Seizure Becomes Legal

In malevolent synergy, concentrations of drug activity beget large numbers of guns. Drug dealers, large and small, feel they need guns, lots of guns, not only to protect their turf but also to avoid being robbed by other armed dealers and to enforce agreements in a marketplace without laws. The twin perils of drugs and guns have enticed law enforcement to take extreme measures in areas where drug dealing is rampant.

Police can conduct warrantless sweeps of public housing units in search of drugs and guns with impunity. Between 1993 and 1994, the Chicago Housing Authority conducted a series of sweeps until U.S. District Court Judge Wayne R. Anderson ruled that it must cease because it violated the Fourth Amendment's prohibition of unreasonable search and seizure. Within hours of that ruling, the Clinton administration called for expansion of the police power to frisk anyone in the common areas surrounding public housing projects.[27] Also called for was allowing local police to enter and search public housing apartments if an "exigent" (emergency) situation existed. Mere suspicion of illegal guns or narcotics constituted such an emergency.[28] Meanwhile, honest, hard-working, drug-free Americans are expected to agree to these sweeps.

## Whose Civil Liberties Are Paramount, the Mother's or the Infant's?

How far can and should society go to protect the unborn fetus from drug abuse by its mother? A study published in *The New England Journal of Medicine* in 1993 reported that over 5 percent of 30,000 California women tested positive for recent drug use just prior to delivery.[29] A 1993 study at Harlem Hospital showed that 10 percent of the babies born there tested positive for illicit drugs.[30]

During a debate on mother/fetus rights, Louise Bishop, a member of the Pennsylvania House of Representatives, asked, "Where do we draw the line? Should smoking, drinking alcohol, exposing oneself to contaminants in the workplace, or staying on one's feet too long also be subject to criminal penalty?"[31] The ACLU, with palpable sarcasm, asked whether pregnant Americans who fly to Europe, exposing their fetuses to increased radiation from the sun, thereby increasing their chances of birth defects, or pregnant women who empty their cat's litter boxes and so risk sudden abortion from the effects of toxoplasmosis, should not also be subject to prosecution.[32]

This conflict over a mother's "right" to use illegal drugs while she is pregnant, versus the state's responsibility to both enforce the drug laws and protect the unborn child, touched off a legal battle in South Carolina. The Medical University of South Carolina (MUSC) noticed a startling increase in the number of drug-involved mothers giving birth to either stillborn babies or infants clearly under the influence of drugs. The staff began ordering drug screening for all pregnant patients in order to obtain an objective measurement of the problem, and within one year, 119 women had tested positive for drugs, all but 15 of whom first visited the hospital at delivery time.[33] All those who tested positive were "counseled and cajoled" to sign up for drug treatment, yet not a single one kept her appointment. Furthermore, of the 15 who came in prior to delivery, only 1 returned for additional prenatal care.

In response to this dismal picture, and with the counsel of Charles Condon, at that time the elected solicitor for Charleston and Berkeley counties (subsequently attorney general of South Carolina), MUSC began informing pregnant drug-positive patients that they would have to participate in drug rehabilitation and test negative on all further drug tests or else face jail and possible loss of their children. MUSC was slapped immediately with a $3 million class-action lawsuit filed by a feminist organization. As a result of charges of racism, since MUSC served a largely black, indigent population, the federal government threatened to withhold funds representing 60 percent of the hospital's budget.[34] The hospital soon abandoned its policy. Charleston women are now in the politically correct position of being free to saturate their fetuses with illegal drugs.

Innocent children born drug-addicted are among the most heart-rending consequences of drug taking. Crack-saturated, mostly premature, underweight, these newborns cause many to oppose the legalization of drugs for this outrage alone. Yet the reality of substance-abusing pregnant women must be faced. In a certain proportion of the child-bearing population, the maternal instinct is lost to mental and physical illness. Under legalization, with wider information and treatment measures, some of these women may get treatment. Unfortunately, many will never voluntarily make themselves available for treatment. Fetal alcohol syndrome has demonstrated this lamentable fact. It is a basic truth that in a democratic society, even a crack-head has rights. But what about the children? Shouldn't their civil rights be taken into consideration, even though their mothers are dysfunctional? Under legalization, this problem should be a top priority. And it is more likely that without the punitive paradigm of prohibition, pregnant users will allow themselves to be more routinely examined. We should have learned by now that we cannot have a country that is both free and free of drugs.

On a brighter note, in a Florida survey, teachers were asked to identify students in their class who had been exposed to drugs before birth. Researchers knew which children had suffered such exposure, but the teachers guessed wrong.[35] Ira J. Chasnoff, president of the National Association for Perinatal Addiction Research and Education in Chicago, disputes the popular notion that cocaine-exposed children represent a "biological underclass" that will challenge school systems beyond capacity.[36] A research paper cited in the *Brown University Digest of Addiction Theory and Application* reported on a six-year study of many aspects of language skills development, including reading and writing, of 26 children exposed prenatally to crack or cocaine. The study reported encouragingly normal development.[37] Neither of these studies supports the widely held notion that such use dooms the child to a lifetime of underachievement.

# 7

———◦◦◦◦———

# THE INUNDATION OF OUR POLICE, COURTS AND PRISONS

It is the nature, indeed the purpose, of democratic institutions to respond to the will of the people. Fueled by the nation's revulsion over the twin tyrannies of drugs and crime, the U.S. has been on a 25-year binge of arrests, indictments, trials, and harsh sentences, all aimed at the impossible goal of stamping out the scourge of drugs and the crime it breeds. Law enforcement agencies estimate that over half of today's crimes are drug-related.[1] Over 1 million Americans each year are arrested for drug offenses, but that is only the tip of the iceberg. Many crimes not classified as drug-related are committed to finance the purchase of illicit drugs; as well as countless murders over drug turf. Separate studies in Miami and New York City, done in 1982 and 1984, respectively, found that 24 percent of all homicides there were drug-related, though not all were originally reported as drug crimes.[2]

With pressure from the body politic about drug-connected crime, we have flooded our courts with drug defendants because, as befits any democratic institution, the judiciary responds to that pressure. Proof of this responsiveness is found in statistics that reveal arrests for drug offenses up a substantial 25 percent between 1986 and 1991, while persons imprisoned for drug offenses in that period increased an astronomical 327 percent.[3]

## Drug Law History

A distinguished Southern California jurist and drug law reformer, Judge James P. Gray, with his tongue firmly in his cheek, has

[98]

compared our drug laws to an aging grandfather: "When my grandfather turned seventy, he started walking three miles a day. He's now seventy-five and we have no idea *where* he is!"

The "grandfather" of American drug law is the Harrison Narcotics Act, passed in 1914. It was meant by the U.S. Congress essentially to ensure adequate record keeping, and was passed largely to fulfill U.S. obligations as a signatory to the International Conference on Opium held at the Hague in 1912.[4] China, the instigator of the conference, experiencing major problems from the proliferation of opium usage within its borders, wanted other nations profiting from the opium trade to pass controlling legislation. The United States, not seriously involved in the opium trade but seeking to improve trade relations with China, attended the conference and subsequently passed the Harrison Act to show its good faith and friendship. Prior to the Harrison Narcotics Act, between the late 1890s and the early 1900s, nearly all the states had already passed laws prohibiting the sale of cocaine, opium, morphine, and heroin without a prescription, but interpretation and enforcement were uneven from state to state. Correcting this inconsistency was also a major motivating factor in the passage of the Harrison Act.

A subsequent judicial decision turned this innocuous piece of legislation into a prohibitionist's weapon. In 1919, the Supreme Court, by a narrow 5–4 decision, held that the law's wording, "prescribed in good faith," could not be used to justify the prescription, for addiction maintenance, of any of the proscribed drugs.[5] The court maintained that "mere addiction" did not constitute a disease that warranted treatment. More drug-law making followed, but the 1919 decision breathed judicial life into the drug war.

Few events are less predictable today than a criminal trial. With so many laws in place to protect the rights of the defendant, it is common for the obviously guilty to be set free for some breach of the rules during either the arrest or the trial. Forgotten is the wisdom of Justice Cardozo's 1926 observation that it makes no sense that "the criminal is to go free because the constable has blundered."

In Philadelphia in 1993, a conviction was overturned because the officer didn't wait the prescribed 15 seconds between knocking on a drug dealer's door and breaking it down.[6] In another example, four convicted smuggling accomplices, after what was then the largest heroin seizure in U.S. history, over half a ton, were given three years' probation by a San Francisco court instead of a stiff jail sentence. All because the judge, citing constitutional protections, ruled that the videotaped surveillance of the warehouse where the drugs were stashed was illegal.[7]

When the word of yet another hoodlum getting off the hook hits the news, one can almost hear the collective groan. Part of the public's problem with these results is that it doesn't understand the constitutional reasons for the safeguards of the defendant's rights. Justice may be served by the employment of a necessary protection, but it looks like just another victory for the bad guys. The electronic and print media would perform a great public service if they consistently built into their stories an historic explanation for seemingly irrational judicial decisions. Such a policy would help restore much-needed public confidence in our criminal justice system. This would be a vital public service as a poll of public opinion taken in 1993 demonstrated when it showed the following percentages of respondents expressing confidence in these American institutions:[8]

| | |
|---|---|
| Military | 67 percent |
| Church | 53 percent |
| Police | 52 percent |
| Congress | 19 percent |
| Criminal justice system | 17 percent |

## Plea Bargaining and Judicial Overload

The rampant use of plea bargaining, whereby a defendant can plead guilty to a lesser charge in order to avoid the cost and uncertainty of a trial, is another slippery slope in the judicial system. The device, sometimes used to extract information from one defendant for the prosecution of another, often allows the intelligence contributor to plead guilty to a less-serious charge. The primary motivation for the use of plea bargaining is to reduce terminal overload of the courts.

Tim Wells and William Triplett, in their book *Drug Wars: An Oral History from the Trenches*, begin their chapter "Prosecution, Prison and Punishment" with this statement: "One of the drug war's more appalling statistics is that 95 percent of everyone arrested for distribution or possession of illegal narcotics never go to court on the original charges. 'Plea bargaining,' a judge said recently, 'is as necessary to this system as breathing and eating is to a human being.' "[9]

The authors interviewed a police officer from Washington, D.C., who told an all-too-familiar story of overload and compromise in the D.C. system:

*Last year we made over 16,000 felony arrests . . . but the courts here are only capable of handling 759 felony trials. So, [the defendants] go back to the community, and say, "Yeah, I got arrested for selling crack cocaine, but nothing happened to me." There's a perception on the street that the system is too backed up to try anybody, and the more drug dealers we have clogging the system, the more accurate that perception becomes.*[10]

Plea bargaining is done so routinely that Charles L. Lindner, a past president of the Los Angeles Criminal Bar Association, wrote:

*Plea bargaining is how the criminal justice system gets through the day. The approximately 120 judges assigned to criminal courts cannot try more than a fraction of the 40,000 felony cases filed each year in Los Angeles. For at least two generations, nontrial case settlements have averaged 96–97 percent of all cases filed. A 1 percent drop in settlements effectively creates judicial gridlock.*[11]

The concept of plea bargaining is taken a step further in many jurisdictions where, in the interest of relieving an already overloaded system, prosecutors will not even file a charge unless the offense surpasses a certain size threshold. For example, in San Diego, at the Mexican border, the U.S. Customs Service files only a misdemeanor charge for the smuggling by a first-time offender of less than 125 pounds of marijuana.[12] With marijuana selling for up to $2,500 a pound, that is about a $300,000 misdemeanor, which brings to mind the old Will Rogers bromide that he didn't make jokes, he just watched the government operate and reported what he saw.

Based on a study conducted in the late 1980s, drug expert Peter Reuter, former codirector of the Rand Corporation's Drug Policy Research Center, put the imprisonment risk per transaction of a drug seller who worked two days a week and had 1,000 transactions in a year at 1 in 4,500.[13] The staff of Senator Joseph R. Biden published a study in 1993 that concluded that the odds of being arrested for buying cocaine were somewhere between 1 in 820 and 1 in 1,640.[14] The unhappy fact is that the risk of arrest for buying and selling drugs is remote. Even so, the more than 1,000,000 arrests per year clog the judicial system.

## Federalization and Judicial Overload

Another very real and immediate threat to our already overloaded federal courts is the increasing "federalization" of our legal system. The basic division of labor in our judicial system is that state and local courts handle cases where a breach of only state or local law has taken place, and the federal courts take over where federal law has been broken.

Currently, state and local courts handle well over 95 percent of the 1.1 million drug arrests made each year by the police representing those jurisdictions. Federal drug arrests — the 20,000 or so arrests made each year by the DEA, FBI, and other federal law enforcement agencies — are handled by the federal courts. Recently, however, well-intentioned but misguided federal office holders and bureaucrats have shown an increasing tendency to federalize specific crimes by having legislation passed making a particular offense or combination of offenses a federal crime. If a crime can be made a violation of both local and federal law, it can be tried in either federal court or state and local court. When the Feds deem the state and local courts to be insufficiently harsh in their punishment or too inconsistent in their guilty verdicts, they can step in and prosecute the case. Furthermore, a person convicted and jailed at the state or local level can be retried in federal court for the same crime after completion of the first sentence. Prior conviction can be used as evidence in the new trial. It can also occur that defendants are acquitted at the state or local level, then retried at the federal level for the same offense.

"That can't happen in America," you say. Ask Tina Elliott. She spent one year in jail in 1988 for trying to buy a half kilo of cocaine from an undercover officer in Georgia. After doing her time on the state charge, the 33-year-old first offender returned home to resume raising her five children, only to be rearrested, retried, and sentenced for the same incident, this time to 20 years in federal prison without possibility of parole. The Supreme Court has ruled that the Fifth Amendment's ban on double jeopardy doesn't apply as long as the prosecutions are done separately by federal and state prosecutors.[15]

Joe Renteria was arrested and sentenced by local authorities in Texas for conspiring to buy marijuana and cocaine, served 11 months in jail and then returned home to Southern California, where he was a scriptwriter. His own script took an unexpected twist when he was arrested by federal authorities for the same incident and received an additional five-year prison term. At the sentencing hearing on the federal charge, Judge David Kenyon said:

*The court is very bothered that the government would let this man or anybody go through an entire sentencing in state court on the exact same facts, wait until he's out of prison, he's starting a new life, he's married, he's working, and then announce, "Now we're going to prosecute you on the federal side." There's something wrong about that. No matter what the person does wrong, that too is wrong.*[16]

## Law Enforcement Overload

What makes it possible for a civilization to rise from anarchy is the courage and willingness of about two out of every thousand citizens to don badges and enforce laws. If ever a substantial percentage of the protected citizens decide that the laws, or those who enforce them, are not worthy of respect, civilization will regress.

We see that regression in America today. Disrespect for the law is manifest. Statutes prohibiting narcotics and related drugs are being ignored by a dangerously high percentage of our people. It is estimated that 63 percent of Americans born since 1955 have used illegal drugs at one time or another.[17] Each year, more than 1.1 million of our citizens are arrested for either possession of or trafficking in illicit drugs.

Disrespect for those who enforce our laws can be attributed to the too-frequent instances when drug criminals are seen back on the streets before the ink is dry on the arrest sheet. Such an instance took place in Washington, D.C., in the summer of 1993, as a result of a police crackdown on an open-air drug market in the northeast section of the nation's capital. When a brawl between drug dealers and police ensued, the windshields on two patrol cars were smashed, and several policemen as well as drug dealers received minor injuries. Among those arrested was a young man who, according to a newspaper report, "has faced more than 30 other charges that have not been fully prosecuted since he turned 18, four years ago." Another arrestee had on separate occasions previously been "found guilty of possessing PCP and marijuana . . . and distributing cocaine . . ." A third man had previously done time for drug distribution. All three, along with two others, were released from jail the next day when charges were dropped by the prosecutors in D.C. Superior Court.[18]

## The Outlaw-Hero Myth Versus Law Enforcement

After death or incarceration, those who traffic in drugs are sometimes raised to the status of modern-day Robin Hoods in their communities, a tendency that trivializes the work of law enforcement to the level of the bumbling Sheriff of Nottingham. It also spins the compass of the youth of our cities as they try to pick their way through the minefield of adolescence toward respectable employment. In some quarters, those who break the law seem more respected than those who enforce it.

From 1975 to 1983 Felix Mitchell was a drug dealer of mythical proportions in Oakland, California. He reportedly made between $5 million and $50 million dollars a year, mostly in the heroin business, and is acknowledged to have ordered the deaths of five rival drug dealers during Oakland's 1980 drug war. He was credited also with bringing money and jobs to the ghettos of Oakland and providing jobs for youngsters, albeit mostly as mules and lookouts for his thriving heroin business. In 1983 Mitchell was arrested, tried, and sent to jail for life without the possibility of parole. He was murdered in jail in 1986, stabbed to death by a fellow inmate. "A lavish funeral procession was held in Oakland with a few thousand people along the route and at the church. The casket was drawn by two horses, followed by Rolls Royces and Cadillacs."[19] The impact such adulation had on the youth of Oakland far outweighed their affection for the police.

In too many neighborhoods, the "love your local outlaw syndrome" means that spending time in jail carries little stigma, and even attaches a certain romanticism to going to jail.[20] Often one's stature can be enhanced in the eyes of the young by having spent some time in "the slammer." These twin fictions combine to make the job of law enforcement much tougher. Without the deterrence of stigma, the lure of fast, easy money is too difficult for many youths to resist. It then falls to our police to bring these lawbreakers to the bar of justice — if they can.

## The Thin Blue Line Under Attack

"If they can" is no idle caveat. Police today face a public that is increasingly hostile. Sheriff Sherman Block of Los Angeles told the *L.A. Times* of an incident in February 1993 when two officers in their patrol car witnessed a drive-by shooting. They immediately gave chase, and just as immediately were fired upon by the fleeing suspect. Undeterred, they persisted and, a few blocks down the street, a bystander drew his pistol and shot at them. Moments later they took fire from another passing car. Sheriff Block stated that within a month of that incident, in a single day suspects fired guns at Southern California officers in six separate incidents.

Alienation of a large segment of society from the police is partly explained because a substantial portion of the American public does not feel that drugs should be against the law. The previously mentioned 63 percent of Americans born since 1955 who have used illegal drugs are evidence of a widespread lack of conviction that drugs are a menace to health and safety. It is hardly surprising that large numbers of our citizens look askance at police efforts to stamp out a practice viewed by so many as routine behavior. This disapproval of police intervention often converts into anger, hatred and interference with and attacks on the police. Too often, vigorous law enforcement activity is misinterpreted as police brutality.

Los Angeles Police Department Sgt. Bob Brannon was parked near a fast food restaurant one night in early 1993, when he heard a loud banging noise. He looked up to see a man shooting at him over a brick wall twenty feet away. His assailant pumped three more shots at him before fleeing. Brannon was unhurt in the attack. His squad car was not so fortunate; it took four bullets in the door. "The suspect was black, the neighborhood was black, but this shooting was not about race because Brannon too is black. 'This shooting was about color — the color blue,' Brannon says."[21]

## Victimless Crime

Most of the drug war consists of victimless crimes, greatly complicating the job of law enforcement. When a person commits the crime of buying, selling, possessing, manufacturing, or transporting illicit drugs, there is no individual victim involved. Professor Randy E. Barnett of Chicago-Kent College of Law asks us to pretend for a moment that robbery is likewise a victimless crime.

*If robberies were "victimless" — if there was no victim complaining to the police and testifying at trial — certain unavoidable enforcement problems would develop. . . . The police would have to embark on a program of systematic surveillance. Because they could not simply respond to a robbery victim's complaint as they do at present, the police would have to be watching everywhere and always. Robberies perpetrated in "public" places — on public streets or transportation — might be detected with the aid of sophisticated surveillance equipment located in these public places. Those robberies committed in private places, homes and stores, would require even more intrusive practices. If the police did detect a robbery, they would be the principal witnesses against the defendant at trial. It would be their word against that of the alleged robber. As a practical matter, it would be within their discretion to go forward with the prosecution or not. There would be no victim pressing them to pursue prosecution and potentially questioning any decision they might make to drop the charges or withhold a criminal complaint.[22]*

Barnett describes exactly the position the police are in when making those 1.1 million drug arrests each year.

## Drug War Is Extremely Labor Intensive

In a typical crime against a person or property such as robbery or rape, the crime is committed, the victim reports it and is present to insist on and assist in the prosecution that, if successful, results in the punishment of the offender. In a drug crime, the only practical way the police can prosecute is to witness the crime personally or participate in it. Officers must observe the crime, arrest the perpetrator and assist in the prosecution. Adding to this the requirements of stakeouts and nearby backup provides the recipe for copious quantities of available police personnel, a resource that is sorely needed in other areas of our society.

Many of the arrestees in a large 1993 LSD bust lived in the town of Bolinas, California, the epicenter of a massive police operation designed to shut down an LSD ring. Developed over a four-year period by the California Bureau of Narcotics Enforcement, the case culminated with a buy-bust operation involving 40 grams of LSD in a nearby town. Simultaneously, an estimated 160 officers from 12 state, federal and local law enforcement agencies made arrests in nine other locations. Prior to the grand finale, two female undercover police had made 25 LSD purchases in the case, spending some $120,000 on the drugs alone. No estimate of the total cost of the operation was reported.[23]

The Bureau of Justice Statistics, in a special report on drug enforcement published in 1992 states that over 18,000 local and state police officers are assigned full time to special drug units. That does not include the part-time drug involvement of hundreds of thousands of other police officers. This diversion of police and judicial resources to the impossible task of stamping out drug use is perhaps the greatest source of harm done by illegal drugs, other than human suffering.

Tampa, Florida, was the site of a 1992 antidrug operation that on the surface seemed to produce results and therefore justify its enormous cost in police resources. Blatant open-air drug markets had literally taken over some streets in many poor and a few well-off areas of the city, where sellers used lawn chairs, couches and ice chests to assure their comfort. Many were strategically placed beneath trees to provide shade. Bonfires burned in barrels on cooler nights. Debris from the fires as well as trash from eating and drinking littered the areas. Buyers flocked to these sources of illicit drugs, feeling secure in the very size and scope of the markets. The Tampa Police Department counted 141 of these "dope holes," as it called them.

Bob Smith, Tampa's public safety administrator, had nightmares about the problem. He said, "You begin to question your own ability; you say, 'Maybe we can't lick this, maybe this is bigger than our police department.'" Smith met with the police leadership to plan a response, and operation QUAD, "Quick Uniformed Attack on Drugs," was born. Forty of Tampa's 750 officers were assigned full time to the project.

The expenditure of huge amounts of police time and effort did bring some results.

*One set of officers posed as dealers, another videotaped the transactions from under cover, another swooped in to arrest buyers and seize vehicles. The buy would go down, the bust team would come and arrest them and haul them off, pick up the tape and evidence; the secretary would be back there at the command post (a large motor home complete with stenographer, property room and vehicle-processing room) typing up the report, another guy would be processing the evidence, another would be interviewing the prisoner, another processing the car. End of the day we'd have what looked like a parking lot full of cars. A typical one-shift operation netted 30 to 45 people and almost as many vehicles. (Most vehicles were returned to their owners for a negotiated price; one unfortunate buyer lost and bought back his panel truck three separate times.)*"[24]

Less than a year and a half after its inception, QUAD had done what it was designed to do. The open-air drug markets were all but nonexistent in Tampa. But before every city replicates this innovative approach, let's take a closer look at the facts. The National Institute of Justice said: "It is worth noting that the Tampa police make no claim to have reduced drug use significantly in the city." Moreover, the index of serious crimes for the state of Florida during operation QUAD experienced a modest rise of 4 percent while Tampa's nearby neighbor, St. Petersburg, endured a whopping 18 percent rise in serious crime. Combined with Tampa's 9 percent drop, this argues strongly that the problems "solved" at such great cost of police resources in Tampa simply moved to St. Petersburg. The operation's long-term impact was insignificant.

When drug operations involve foreign countries, more police manpower and money are demanded. "Operation Bamboo Dragon," with heroin as the principal product, involved perpetrators from Hong Kong. The list of government organizations assigned to the case in the early 1990s reads like a federal law enforcement directory: the FBI; the Bureau of Alcohol, Tobacco, and Fire Arms; the U.S. Customs Service; the Immigration and Naturalization Service; and the Washington, D.C., Metropolitan Police.

In 1993, the strain of drug-related operations on the police resources of Los Angeles and Washington, D.C., grew so grave that there were cries to call out the National Guard. During the long, hot summer, in an Op-Ed piece in the *Los Angeles Times*, a popular talk-show host told of his experience when he picked up on a Los Angeles city councilman's suggestion to bring in the Guard to secure the streets and asked his listeners for comments. "I got a sea of lights flashing across my board, as callers one after another voiced support for the notion of bringing in the 'cavalry.' . . . But why was I surprised? Who can deny that we have a security crisis?"[25]

The cry for the guard in D.C. came from higher up the political ladder during that same summer. Mayor Sharon Pratt Kelley wrote directly to President Clinton asking permission to call up the D.C. National Guard, as governors are allowed to do in times of crisis. Mayor Kelley alleged that many citizens of the city had asked her to do so to restore peace to their drug-infested streets. Since military personnel may not make civilian arrests or searches, President Clinton rejected Mayor Kelley's request but did make available some police assets from the U.S. Capitol Police and the U.S. Secret Service. The skirmish was won, but Washington, with one of the highest murder rates in the United States — one third of them drug-related — is still a city under siege.[26]

Another example of the price we are paying for waging the drug war is that a brisk market has developed in our largest cities, mostly among recent immigrants, in the illegal sale of prescription drugs. Untrained, unlicensed tailgate druggists sell smuggled prescription drugs in bakeries, butcher shops and even at swap meets. These illegal operators sell everything from powerful heart medications to capsules of penicillin "while overextended authorities do virtually nothing to stop them. . . . State and federal agencies say they do not have the resources . . . to mount a serious challenge to the black market."[27] Clearly, this drug problem is deserving of the attention of our law enforcement resources, but does not get that attention, simply because the enforcers are too preoccupied with the "real" drug war.

Time and other resources expended on drug crimes are unavailable for cases of rape, murder, and extortion. Drug cases so disproportionately absorb police time, prosecutors' time, and court slots that shortages result, which encourage plea bargaining, leading to lighter sentences for major criminals and a "revolving door" justice system that releases dangerous, often violent, offenders back among the public quickly.

## Penal System Overload

Even with plea bargaining and overloaded courts releasing drug offenders routinely into their previous lives, prisons are still bursting with convicted drug offenders. A letter to *The New York Times* provides some wry humor about drug incarceration:

> *Senator Phil Gramm tells us in "Don't Let Judges Set Crooks Free" (Op-Ed July 8, 1993) that each extra year of imprisonment saves $430,000 in crime and that this return on investment is "a brilliant allocation of resources." If the Senator is right, he has solved the Federal deficit. The number of Americans behind bars in 1993 is about 700,000 greater than in 1980. At $430,000 per capita, we are now saving $300 billion a year through extra prison and jail use. This leads to two questions. Where is the money? And is Senator Gramm always this silly, or does criminal justice policy bring out the worst in him?*

As of late 1993, 40 states were under court order to end prison overcrowding.[28] According to the Bureau of Justice Statistics, at the end of 1996 the federal prison system was operating at 25 percent over its capacity. State prisons were running at 16 to 24 percent over their capacity.[29] Although the growth rate slowed some in 1996, between 1985 and 1996 the average annual growth of the prison population was 8.1 percent.[30] At that rate of growth the prison population will double in less than nine years.

A second force has joined the huge increase in drug arrests to deluge our prisons: the get-tough-on-drugs attitude of our judiciary. According to a 1993 report by the American Bar Association, "The number of persons imprisoned is increasing three times faster than adult arrests, [while] the number **imprisoned for drug offenses** is increasing thirteen times faster than adult drug arrests (emphasis added).[31]

The ratio of inmates to corrections officers in our prisons and jails is growing steadily in favor of the inmates, as we are occasionally reminded by a bloody prison riot somewhere. In 1989, the nation-wide ratio was 4.7 inmates to each officer.[31] By 1996, the ratios of Ohio and California, among the highest in the nation, had risen to 6.1 to 1 and 7.3 to 1, according to statistics from the American Correctional Association.

Even so, the cost of incarceration per year per prisoner rose from about $15,000 in 1987 to $20,000 in 1992, a 33 percent increase.[33] Prison construction also added to costs. Between 1984 and 1990, prison capacity increased an astounding 60 percent. That's the good news. The bad news is that by the end of 1996 state prisons were operating at 16–24 percent above capacity, and federal prisons at 25 percent over capacity.[34]

## Alternatives to Prison

When prisons are overcrowded and budgets correspondingly con-strained, job training, education, and drug treatment are given short shrift. The result: prison recidivism is high. Senator Joseph R. Biden Jr., in the introduction to his committee's April 1993 publication, *America's Drug Strategy*, asserted that from 1990 to 1993, "at least 1,000,000 drug-addicted offenders were released from prison with-out being treated."

It has been established that drug treatment forced upon the user is no less effective than voluntary treatment.[35] While this may sound inherently improbable, it is surely a function of the content and approach of the treatment program. It is also well proven that the cost of treatment is a bargain we cannot afford to ignore. For every dollar spent on treatment, the savings in social costs are $11.54.[36] That's a return on investment hard to match in any endeavor, public or private. Drug treatment for drug-involved inmates is certainly an opportunity to curb the soaring rates of recidivism.

The probation system, like parole and plea bargaining, can

metamorphose into a tool of expediency and injustice when it is used to relieve the overload of the judicial and prison systems, as noted by Attorney General Janet Reno: "With many state prison systems being forced to release inmates early and the federal system at capacity, many major drug figures are serving only a fraction of their sentences."[37] Still, probation, in use since since its first formal program was created in Boston in 1878, has been constructively used in Oregon in a program dubbed DROP, for Drug Reduction of Probationers. Probationers who fail a routine mandatory drug test earn a two-day jail sentence the first time, 10 days the second time, and 30 days the third. Formal assessment and drug treatment accompany the testing. After the third jail sentence, less than 6 percent of the probationers test positive again.[38] Oregon has used DROP not only to punish lawbreakers, but also to force-feed them society's values. The truism that you can lead a horse to water but you can't make it drink has Oregon betting that at least you can keep it from death by dehydration.

Twenty-six states currently operate a total of 57 so-called "boot camps" with a capacity of 8,800 inmates. With facilities similar to armed forces basic training camps, these alternatives to prison stress fitness, job training, high school equivalency classes, and of course drug education and rehabilitation. There are two federally run boot camps with a capacity of about 300.[39]

In 1993, Dade County, Florida, where Attorney General Janet Reno was once prosecutor and purportedly started the program called Drug Court, treatment instead of prison became the answer to first-time nonviolent drug offenders. After four years, the program had diverted 3200 graduates from Florida's prison system. They obtained strictly monitored treatment, regular urine tests and counseling. First offenders who successfully complete the program have their arrest expunged from their records. Drug Court costs about $600 per offender per year.[40] Boot Camp and Drug Court, like the Oregon probation program, offer the justice system ingenious alternatives for first-time nonviolent drug offenders.

## Treatment as an Option

A report written by staffs of the Senate Judiciary Committee and the International Narcotics Control Caucus had this to say about treatment for drug offenders:

> *Research on drug treatment programs has confirmed that addicts are one-tenth to one-third as likely to commit crime while they are in treatment, and less than one-half as likely to have returned to drug abuse and crime one year after leaving treatment. Some of the leading studies have indicated that even drug offenders who are* **forced** *to enroll in treatment are really as likely to stay off drugs and away from crime as those addicts who enter treatment voluntarily (emphasis added).*[41]

The three basic types of treatment programs — methadone maintenance (mostly outpatient), residential treatment and outpatient nonmethadone programs — vary greatly in content and results. Methadone is an oral drug that allows heroin users to withdraw from their addiction without going through the throes of withdrawal. One dose of methadone is nonintoxicating and frees the addict from opiate-craving anxiety for 24 to 36 hours. The objective of a methadone program is to move the addict to total abstinence, but some take longer than others to achieve this goal. Some never make it. However, the Federal Office of Technology Assessment, in a 1990 study, judged methadone to be a safe and effective means of treatment, and found that a substantial majority of those who enter methadone treatment experience a reduction in drug use and criminality and an improvement in health.[42]

Unfortunately, most judges, having seen so many relapsed drug offenders, are loath to use treatment as an alternative to incarceration. It is vital that the drug treatment community reach out to the judiciary and tell its story convincingly to assure that treatment is more seriously considered, especially in cases of first-time, non-violent offenders.

Drug treatment, perhaps the best alternative to the overload of our criminal justice, judicial and penal systems, is scarce. By its nature, treatment is an uncertain, relapse-ridden enterprise, and one in which many jurisdictions are unwilling to place their monies. Even when 14 Manhattan Criminal Court judges urged treatment instead of a jail sentence for New York's nonviolent drug users, funding for even a single staff member was not forthcoming.[43] Every residential or outpatient program for drug treatment suffers from the same malady: insufficient resources.

Yet a 1990 study by the National Association of State Alcohol and Drug Abuse Directors found that drug treatment costs between $2,300 and $14,600 per person per year, whereas incarceration costs between $25,000 and $50,000 per person per year. A May 1997 editorial in the *Los Angeles Times* pointed out, further:

> *A growing body of research shows that such programs effectively reduce recidivism rates. A recent study by the National Development and Research Institute, for instance, found that within two years after being released from prison, 65 percent of untreated substance-abusing convicts were rearrested, compared to only 16 percent of convicts treated in an intensive substance abuse program.*[44]

Another promising idea to attack recidivism is the requirement that an inmate pass a GED (General Educational Development) high school equivalency test before being granted parole or any time off for good behavior. A moment's reflection on the chance for gainful employment of an ex-convict without even a high school diploma, drives home the obvious wisdom of this idea. The only question is: "Why isn't it already the law in all 50 states?"

Today, our nation's drug treatment capacity is over 1,000,000 beds short of serving those who could benefit. A reassessment of spending priorities — from the interdiction and incarceration of our present war on drugs to the education and treatment possible under controlled distribution — would be one of the most benign yet powerful solutions to our drug problem.

# 8

## RACE RELATIONS AND DRUGS: A GRIM PROSPECT

Prior to our national preoccupation with the war against illicit drugs, some improvement in race relations had led Americans to expect accelerating progress toward a color-blind society, as they contemplated the strides made since the passage of the Civil Rights Act of 1964. Clear evidence of progress can be found in an opinion poll conducted by National Opinion Research Center (NORC) of the University of Chicago.[1] NORC had asked the same questions of the white population over three decades.

1. Do you think white students and black students should go to the same or separate schools?

|  | 1956 | 1968 | 1985 | 1996 |
|---|---|---|---|---|
| Same schools | 49% | 73% | 93% | * |
| Separate schools | 51% | 27% | 7% | |

*Because of the near unanimity of opinion in 1985, NORC dropped this question from subsequent surveys.

2. [Do you think] white people have a right to keep black people out of their neighborhoods, [and that] black people should respect that right?

|  | 1963 | 1977 | 1989 | 1996 |
|---|---|---|---|---|
| Agree | 61% | 42% | 23% | 12% |
| Disagree | 39% | 58% | 77% | 88% |

3. If your political party nominated a black person for president, would you vote for that person if he or she were qualified?

|     | 1958 | 1967 | 1989 | 1996 |
| --- | --- | --- | --- | --- |
| Yes | 37% | 53% | 81% | 92% |
| No | 63% | 47% | 19% | 8% |

4. Do you think there should be laws against marriages between blacks and whites?

|     | 1963 | 1968 | 1989 | 1996 |
| --- | --- | --- | --- | --- |
| Yes | 61% | 55% | 23% | 12% |
| No | 39% | 45% | 77% | 88% |

## The Growing Black Underclass

The NORC study suggests that from 1989, there should have been an increase in blacks and whites living together harmoniously in integrated neighborhoods. But this did not happen, nor is it happening today. Urban black ghettos are fiery reminders that, in spite of gains in education, housing and jobs, in spite of evidence that the black working poor and the middle and upper classes are no more involved with drugs than their counterparts among other races, an ominous and growing presence, the black underclass, has emerged. This group, the source for most of black America's drug use and trafficking, and the crimes that go with them, has come to experience residential isolation; increasingly, its children are fatherless, and become school dropouts with no work experience. A disproportionate number of its members are behind bars. These desperate people have hardened the perception of the rest of society toward African Americans in general, raining disdain and prejudice on the undeserving heads of millions of honest, hard-working people and reversing decades of hard-won progress in race relations.

Justice Department studies into drug-related emergency-room visits provide insight into the racial distribution of problematic drug involvement. While blacks represent about 12 percent of America's population they account for 28 percent of drug-related emergency-room visits nationwide and 40 percent of all drug arrests.[2]

In their insightful book *American Apartheid*, sociologists Douglas S. Massey and Nancy A. Denton examine the ghettoization phenomenon in depth:

> *By isolating blacks in racially homogeneous neighborhoods and concentrating poverty within them, segregation creates an environment where failure to meet the ideal standards of American society loses its stigma. . . . The force of oppositional culture is particularly powerful among African Americans because it is so strongly reinforced by residential segregation.*[3]

The residential segregation of the black underclass and the resulting concentration of drug activity in inner-city America are prime contributors to the mistaken perception that the drug war is racially inspired — that, in fact, it is a war on black Americans. Because so many blacks live in high-density urban settings, perfect for the predations of drug dealers, it is inevitable that blacks are disproportionately caught up in the drug trade.

It is clear that police, faced with the job of combating drug-related crime, are drawn to the inner-city landscape. What hunter would not prefer to have his quarry out in the open in a concentrated setting? Charles Ramsey, head of the Chicago police narcotics division, has said:

> *There's as much cocaine in the Sears Tower or in the Stock Exchange as there is in the black community. But those deals are harder to catch. Those deals are done in office buildings, in somebody's home, and there's not the violence associated with it that there is in the black community. But the guy standing on*

*the corner, he's almost got a sign on his back. These guys are just arrestable.*[4]

## Crack and Its Racial Consequences

Race was not a major issue in the drug war until the advent of crack cocaine. Since crack's introduction in the early 1980s, it has done more to worsen race relations than any other aspect of the war on drugs. Some black defendants charged with selling crack cocaine have claimed that their indictments were the result of racially selective prosecution.

At the time of its introduction, a piece of crack cocaine could be bought for as little as $5, whereas the minimum buy of regular cocaine was 10 to 20 times that amount. Consequently, crack became immediately alluring to the poor. Because of the low price and the intensity of its effect when smoked, crack was a tremendous success for the nation's drug dealers. Its use spread like an epidemic, frightening a well-intentioned Congress in 1986 into quickly passing laws mandating sentences as much as 100 times greater for crack than for powdered cocaine. The rationale was that by hitting crack with a sledgehammer, the United States could stop its spread and save the nation from this demon drug. But such a short time elapsed from the recognition of the threat to the passage of the draconian laws that only after the fact did it become clear that selling crack was an almost exclusively black enterprise. The apparently racist laws were already on the books and our leaders lacked the political courage to remove them.

A report issued by the U.S. Sentencing Commission in March of 1995 stated that 88 percent of those charged in federal court with crack offenses were African American. The commission was making the case that the law was inherently racist because it takes 500 grams of powdered cocaine, favored by whites, to result in a five-year mandatory minimum sentence while a mere 5 grams of crack cocaine, favored by blacks, will trigger that same sentence.[5] President

Clinton ignored the U.S. Sentencing Commission's recommendation to soften crack sentences and signed a bill on October 30, 1995, to keep in place the unwise imbalance between sentences.[6] In the spring of 1997, the U.S. Sentencing Commission again recommended bringing the sentences closer together.[7] This time the Clinton administration's initial reaction was more positive, but by early 1998, it had still taken no action.

Since drug sellers are in violation of both local and federal laws, federal prosecutors can pick cases they wish to prosecute and leave the rest to the local prosecutors. Federal practice has been to prosecute the more serious cases, that is, drug sales, and leave simple possession to the local authorities. Because the selling of crack is so dominated by blacks, the result is the appearance of selective racial prosecution by the Feds.

That crack has become an overwhelmingly black phenomenon is demonstrated by some startling statistics. Justice Department statistics show that from 1983 through 1989, the percentage of adults arrested for drug violations who were black rose from 31.5 to 41.5.[8] Did our law enforcement people suddenly become more racist during that period? Clearly not. The change simply reflects the increasingly heavy involvement of the black population with crack.

## Distrust of Government

Grim proof of the corrosive effect of the drug war on the confidence of black America in its government is found in an opinion poll taken among black residents of New York City in 1990. Respondents were shown the statement "Some people say the government deliberately makes sure that drugs are easily available in poor, black neighborhoods in order to harm black people." They were then asked to select from the following options: "Do you think it is true?" (25 percent did); "It might possibly be true" (35 percent); "Almost certainly not true" (34 percent).[9] For 60 percent of the respondents to think the statement was either certainly or possibly true is a serious indictment of black America's confidence in its government.

There is no doubt that the reason for this suspicion is that the drug problem hits the black community disproportionately. African-American assessment of the drug problem differs from that of the population at large. The black community is more critical of its failures. It is harder hit by drugs' collateral damage; and it has suffered more casualties per capita as a result of the war on drugs. Andrew Cooper, the publisher of Brooklyn's black newspaper *City Sun*, has said, "It's a deep-seated suspicion. I believe it. I can't open my desk drawer and say, 'Here it [the evidence] is.' But there is just too much money in narcotics. People really believe they are being victimized by The Man. If the government wanted to stop it, it could stop it."[10]

## Prison Population Disproportionately African American

Another bone of contention that black America gnaws on is the incarceration rate of blacks, which, according to Bureau of the Census figures, is over six times higher than for whites. Of every 100,000 blacks, 965 are in prison; of every 100,000 whites, 155 are. The highest ratio occurs in Minnesota, where there are 19 blacks in jail for every white inmate.

Throughout U.S. history the imprisonment rate was fairly stable until the onset of the vigorous prosecution of the drug war. Since 1980, the nation's prison and jail population has more than trebled, from just over 500,000 inmates to about 1,600,000 in 1996. During the same period, drug arrests grew at a slightly lower annual rate, from 470,000 in 1980 to over 1.1 million by 1995. Not only are more drug offenders going to prison, they're getting longer sentences. The average sentence served for a federal drug offense is now 60 months, compared to 23 months in 1987.[11] These figures, combined with the high percentage of drug arrests involving blacks (41.5 percent), result in an alarmingly high black incarceration rate.

Separate studies in Missouri and Pennsylvania show that African-American judges are more likely than their white peers to incarcerate black juvenile arrestees. In 1993, a black Philadelphia judge revoked a 14-year-old offender's probation and had him incarcerated because he was not attending school. Civil libertarians were outraged. The judge's answer: "What hope is there for a black boy in America without an education? At least in custody he must go to classes. Maybe, just maybe, he will get on track."[12]

From Chicago comes the story of a judge who went against the recommendations of both the probation officer and the prosecuting attorney when he incarcerated a black youngster guilty of a relatively minor offense. The boy's mother had changed the judge's mind from the normal course of complying with those recommendations. She had pleaded with the judge to lock her son up because she feared for his life if he were released back to the neighborhood. She said, "He will die! He'll be dead if you let him out."[13]

Lacking precise measurement, our fairest answer to racism's role in the startlingly high percentage of black prisoners is provided by the studies of Dean Alfred Blumstein of Carnegie-Mellon and Joan Petersilia of the Rand Corporation, which conclude that about 80 percent of the black over-representation in prison can be explained by differential involvement in crime and about 20 percent by subsequent racially discriminatory processes.[14]

Unlike Asian immigrants, who also have a heavy dose of racial enmity to swallow but have succeeded dramatically in America, African-Americans still suffer from their perception of animosity and discrimination from the rest of the country. The black underclass in particular, aided by many black leaders, has adopted the role of victim. African-American intellectual and political leaders (with a few notable exceptions) need to replace their calls for subsidy, preference and advantage with positive leadership and a call for their people's return to the fundamental principles of family, education and hard work. By eliminating the option of drug dealing as an alternative to the honest labor upon which society depends, America can get back on track toward racial equality and integration. We are yet an imperfect nation, but by standing down from the war on drugs, we can put its racial suspicions and injustices, real and imagined, behind us and get on with the business of making America a more color-blind society.

# 9

## AIDS AND DRUGS

AIDS (Acquired Immune Deficiency Syndrome) was first diagnosed in 1981. Since then, 612,000 Americans have been reported to the Centers for Disease Control and Prevention as having had the disease; by June 30, 1997, 397,258 people had died.[1] David Satcher, U.S. Surgeon General, has said, "In the history of epidemics, AIDS is among the worst in the world. In December of 1984, three fourths of AIDS cases were men who have sex with men. This year [1994], this group makes up only a little more than half of all cases." Increasingly, AIDS victims are injection-drug users (IDUs) and their sexual partners.[2]

   While rumors and contradictions abound, so far the only two clinically proven ways to transmit HIV (the human immunodeficiency virus, which causes AIDS), are through blood or semen. The trace amounts of blood left on a hypodermic needle provide the deadly bridge for virus transmission from one IDU to another. Over one third of AIDS cases diagnosed since 1988 are the direct result of either needle sharing or sexual contact with IDUs. This includes heterosexuals, homosexuals, and children born of infected mothers.[3]

### Gay Men, Needle Sharing

The leading cause of AIDS among gay men is unprotected sexual activity. In addition, approximately one third of all gay men are chemically dependent.[4] It is unclear just how the dependencies break down between drugs and alcohol, but it can be assumed that drug abuse is as common as alcoholism. As with other populations of IDUs, needle sharing among gay men is prevalent. Nearly all IDUs admit to sharing a needle at least once.[5] In an otherwise grim picture, however, the gay community has shown considerable vigor in attacking the dangerous practice of needle sharing. Needle exchange programs, both legal and illegal, have been established in dozens of communities across the country to exchange clean needles for used ones and thereby reduce or eliminate the IDU's inclination to share, often a part of the first injection experience. Once a gay male becomes HIV-positive, he can become a Typhoid Mary times two, spreading the disease both through unprotected sexual activity and needle sharing. Because of HIV's long incubation period, carriers are sometimes unaware they are infected. The Centers for Disease Control (CDC) estimated in 1997 that 275,000 Americans were unaware that they were HIV-positive.[6]

A terrifying example of the spread of HIV by needle sharing is revealed by a study conducted by the CDC. It traced the spread of HIV from one Berks County, Pennsylvania, prisoner who was known to be an IDU and discovered that he had AIDS. Over a 16-month study period following the diagnosis, the state's Department of Health identified 142 people linked to him by sex or shared needles either directly or through someone else. By carefully tracking those 142 unsuspecting people, the department was able to contact all but 3. Blood tests established that 50 of those contacted (36 percent) were infected with the HIV virus. Ensuring that the tragedy was in the process of being extended infinitely, 24 of the infected 50 did not know they had the virus until the study found them.[7]

## IDUs: Their Numbers and Habitats

Estimates of the number of people in the United States who regularly inject heroin, cocaine, and other illicit drugs range from 1,100,000 to 1,500,000.[8] Because heroin is the drug of choice of the majority of IDUs, the words "drugs" and "heroin" are used interchangeably in this discussion.

New York and San Francisco share the dubious distinction of

being America's AIDS epicenters, home to over 25 percent of the nation's AIDS patients.[9] The two cities have large populations of gays and IDUs. Much of the injection activity in poor areas takes place in rooms in abandoned hotels and rooming houses called shooting galleries. These concentrations of high-HIV-risk behavior are frequented by addicted prostitutes seeking drugs for sex, both gay and straight addicts looking for ready access to drugs, dope peddlers, and assorted hangers-on.

In the early 1990s, local police of the Bushwick area of Brooklyn were keenly aware of the shooting galleries in their precincts, and periodic police invasions resulted in hundreds of arrests in a single day. However, these forays had unintended consequences. "The effect of a police occupation just drives the addicts and dealers to other neighborhoods and increases the spread of HIV and tuberculosis," said Sam Friedman, principal investigator for the National Development Research Institute, a private agency that studies drug policy.[10] About 60 percent of IDUs in New York City and 15 percent in San Francisco are HIV-positive.[11]

## The Need for the Needle

Estimates of the percentage of illicit drug users who end up as IDUs vary from 1.5 to 2.0 percent — over a million people in the United States.[12]

Given that a certain number of people are driven by their own personal demons to take heroin, the logical mind still asks, "Why take it by injection, with all its attendant dangers?" If one is addicted, why not smoke it, snort it, or eat it? Or why not use another of the many narcotics available like morphine, codeine, barbiturates, or quaaludes? Those are logical questions, but IDUs are not logical people.

Several studies have demonstrated that the act of injecting and the lifestyle surrounding it are important components in an IDU's addiction. During the early 1960s, a group of 91 heroin addicts emigrated from Canada to Britain to escape the crackdown on heroin use in their own country. They enrolled in a British program that provided pure heroin at no cost to the addict. Only 25 of them found the program satisfactory and remained in Britain. Those who returned to Canada frequently reported that they "missed the street scene" and did not get the same high from pure, clinically administered heroin as from the adulterated street product they injected themselves.[13] Another study of addicts found that "the single prick of a needle or the hypodermic injection of sterile water" alleviated withdrawal symptoms.[14] It is clear that an IDU's addiction is not purely pharmacological.

Dr. Andrew Weil and Winifred Rosen, in *From Chocolate to Morphine*, their book on mind-altering drugs, describe the heroin addict: "Visible addicts tend to be in trouble, involved with crime, in poor health, purposeless, psychologically damaged, unhappy and unable to get out of their grim predicaments."[15] Both the ritual of needle use and the drug-seeking lifestyle surrounding it are major elements of psychological impairment. IDUs who are not mentally impaired engage in denial of risk and reality, part of which is a widespread refusal to seek or accept treatment. Less than 25 percent of IDUs are in treatment at any one time. About half of IDUs, when asked whether they would enter treatment if it were available, say they would decline.[16]

The following is an exchange between two IDUs recorded by a reporter in Bushwick, Brooklyn:

*"Yo, yo, yo, baby, I borrow your works?" She warns: "Honey I got the HIV." Ceaser shrugs; annoyed almost. "That's why they invented bleach, right?" He takes her syringe, draws up a tumbler full of bleach, squirts it out, fills it again with heated heroin and jams it into his elbow. No one would tell him that's safe; bleach needs at least a minute and a half to kill the*

*virus — if it kills it at all. Ceaser looks up, shoulders huge and pockmarked. "I'm going back to prison. Who the hell cares if I'm HIV positive?"*[17]

## IDU-Related AIDS and Minorities

When one third of all the AIDS cases in the United States (caused by being an IDU or having unprotected sex with one) are broken down ethnically, among the African-American population, 52 percent of AIDS cases are IDU-related; among Hispanics, 45 percent; among whites, 19 percent.[18]

It is discouraging to note that the drug conspiracy theory held by some in the black community has caused African Americans to vigorously oppose Needle Exchange Programs (NEPs). In 1993, researchers from the School of Public Health at the University of California reported: "The most consistent source of opposition to needle exchange programs were African-American church and community leaders."[19] One of the reasons these leaders cited was their fear that needle exchange might encourage drug use. In the minds of some black leaders, the feared increase in drug use among blacks amounted to genocide.[20]

## Needle Exchange Programs: History

Compared to America, the drug debate in most European countries focuses much less on criminality and punishment. For the most part, the European approach focuses on harm reduction. Peter Reuter, formerly head of Rand Corporation's Drug Policy Research Center, offers this observation:

> *The health consequences [of drug use] dominate discussion in most of Europe. . . . Syringe exchange schemes . . . have become common in Britain, the Netherlands, Italy, and the German cantons of Switzerland. Spain and the Netherlands, with*

*very different social policies toward drug use generally, have given the criminal law a minor role in dealing with drug users. As the Advisory Council on the Misuse of Drugs in Great Britain said in a 1988 report, "HIV is a greater threat to public and individual health than drug misuse."* [21]

The first needle exchange program opened in Amsterdam in 1984. Shortly thereafter, under Margaret Thatcher's conservative government, NEPs were legalized in the United Kingdom.

The public health approach to drug-related AIDS was first implemented in the Mersey region of England. Armed with the philosophy that AIDS prevention should take precedence over drug abuse because AIDS is the greater threat to the drug user, the public health and the national economy, now the Mersey area has the highest rate in England of drug users receiving treatment. It also boasts the lowest number of HIV-positive drug users in England.[22] Liverpool, a huge seaport within the Mersey region, has many prostitutes and a high rate of drug use, but the HIV infection rate for Liverpool IDUs is .1 percent, compared to about 60 percent in New York City.[23]

By 1986, the NEPs idea crossed the Atlantic and two programs were introduced, illegally, in New Haven and Boston. The idea quickly spread, and in 1988, Tacoma, Washington, established the first legal NEP to offer comprehensive services, including referral to treatment.

As of September 1993 there were 37 NEPs operating in 30 cities throughout the United States.[24] That number had grown to 68 by 1996.[25] About 40 percent of them were legal, and of those that were illegal, about half were tolerated and purposely ignored by local law enforcement. During 1993 alone, NEPs distributed about 2 million sterile syringes, most of them in exchange for used ones.[26]

Further evidence of the importance of easy access to clean needles is that IDUs who are also diabetic, and therefore have ready access to clean needles for insulin injection, experience a much lower incidence of HIV. A Baltimore study found a 2.5 times higher rate of HIV among nondiabetic IDUs compared to diabetic injectors.[27]

In 1994, the American Academy of Pediatrics, concerned about the growing number of children born with AIDS, appointed a task force to examine methods of prevention. Despite all the rhetoric against public support for NEPs, the task force from this professional organization issued a policy statement declaring that such programs can go a long way toward preventing the disease among both children and adolescents.[28]

Because of the accumulation of this kind of evidence, there is a realization dawning that such laws and policies against NEPs are both counterproductive and inhumane. On June 26, 1994, Kristine Gebbie, the White House AIDS policy coordinator, told the AIDS Task Force for the U.S. Conference of Mayors that state and local governments should begin NEPs without waiting for federal assistance or urging.[29] Maine and Connecticut were the first states to change their laws and make NEPs legal.

Most of the progress on legalizing NEPs has been at the city level. In 1993, in San Francisco, Mayor Frank Jordan, who as a former chief of police in that city had vigorously enforced needle laws, became so alarmed at the spread of AIDS among IDUs after he became mayor that he declared a state of emergency in the city. With the support of the city council he legalized and then funded a formerly underground NEP.

Following San Francisco's example, Philadelphia's Board of Health declared a state of emergency and agreed to circumvent state law and authorize NEPs in that city. In New York City, Mayor David Dinkins heeded mounting evidence of the efficacy of NEPs and reversed his previous stand against them in 1993. Utilizing an emergency waiver from the state board of health, he launched four new pilot programs among that city's IDUs, who, as previously noted, have a catastrophic 60 percent rate of HIV infection.[30] Mayor Richard Riordan of Los Angeles tried to jump on the state-of-emergency bandwagon but a recalcitrant county counsel deemed the move illegal. Consequently, the City of Angels limps along with several underground NEPs. Using a slightly different approach, Chicago found an obscure provision in its state law that allowed the possession of needles for research purposes.[31]

As a means of needle distribution, NEPs are superior to the suggestion of distribution through pharmacies without a prescription. NEPs typically are open for much longer hours and are more user-friendly. Also, NEPs collect used needles for medical research and distribute free condoms as a sideline.

Perhaps the most edifying and least recognized function of NEPs is as a bridge to drug treatment. Many IDUs are isolated individuals whose repeated contact with the nonjudgmental staff of the NEP is often their only positive connection with the drug-free world. A good example of strong referral activity is in New Haven, where, according to a 1991 report, one quarter of the 720 clients of the exchange program asked for help in overcoming their addiction and over half requested help to enter treatment. Across the continent, Tacoma, Washington's NEP is the biggest single source of referrals to the county's methadone treatment program.[32]

The economics of NEPs are refreshing. The average annual cost of a pilot program ranges from $25,000 to $65,000. Larger, more comprehensive programs like Tacoma's can cost between $100,000 and $200,000 per year.[33] Programs of all sizes rely heavily on volunteers, a major reason why the average cost of operating a NEP for one year compares favorably with the lifetime cost of treating one terminal AIDS patient.

"Paraphernalia" laws exist in 46 states and the District of Columbia, making the manufacture, possession, or distribution of drug-taking equipment illegal, including, of course, hypodermic needles. Prescription laws exist in 10 states, which make possession of needles illegal without a doctor's prescription. There is a clearly demonstrated connection between these laws and the rate of HIV infection among IDUs. Fifteen percent of those entering drug treatment from states that have prescription laws are infected, compared to 3 percent from states without such laws.[34]

The two most common arguments against NEPs are that their legalization sends the wrong message, especially to the young, about drug use, and that to supply clean needles for drug use is to encourage it. What these programs really encourage and condone is acknowledgment that the saving of human lives is one of mankind's most basic responsibilities. That obligation is not removed simply because a human being has a deviant lifestyle. One woman's response to demands for the elimination of the NEP where she volunteered was "It's like saying that if you took away all condoms, people would stop having sex. Not very likely, is it?"

## All Things Considered, Are NEPs a Good Idea?

Mark Twain once observed:

> In the space of 176 years the lower Mississippi has shortened itself 242 miles. . . . Any person can see that 742 years from now the lower Mississippi will be only a mile and three quarters long, and Cairo and New Orleans will have joined their streets together, and be plodding comfortably along under a single mayor and a mutual board of aldermen. There is something fascinating about science. One gets such wholesale returns of conjecture out of such trifling investment of fact.

Similar thinking characterizes today's drug warriors, with their dire predictions that allowing drug addicts access to clean needles will create more addicts. It's pure speculation. A sampling of evidence to the contrary:

1.  A 1992 study by Yale University of a NEP in New Haven showed a 33 percent reduction in the rate of HIV infection among that

cities' IDUs.[35] A year later, the General Accounting Office, the financial watchdog agency, examined the study and reported that "most studies show clean needle programs do not lead to increases in injection drug use among participants."[36] The agency went on to recommend that the government drop its prohibition against funding NEPs.

2. A study published in the *Journal of the American Medical Association* in 1993 of over 5,600 San Francisco IDUs showed that among clients of NEPs the incidence of needle sharing dropped from 66 percent before the NEPs opened to 35 percent after four years of operation.[37] It also reported a drop in the daily frequency of injection from 1.9 times per day to .7, thus dispelling fears that the existence of NEPs might increase the frequency of drug injection.[38]

3. Another study, reported in the same issue of *JAMA*, concerned New York City. In that study of IDUs, the incidence of needle sharing dropped from 51 percent of injections to 7 percent over the two-year period of the study. Dr. Don C. Des Jarlais, head of the Chemical Dependency Institute at Beth Israel Medical Center in New York, attributes the decline partially to the growing use of NEPs during the study period.[39]

4. In a study commissioned by Congress, the Institute of Medicine (IOM) has strongly advocated the removal of the ban on federal funding of NEPs. "The weight of evidence suggests that needle exchange does more good than harm," said H. Keith Brodie, the Duke University researcher who wrote the IOM study.[39]

Beneath all the well-intentioned rhetoric about sending out the wrong message is the cold reality that by keeping needles illegal, society is raising the stakes in the gamble the user takes each time he or she obtains a syringe. Those who, for good moral and ethical reasons, oppose NEPs should get the message that while injecting drugs is destructive and distasteful, it is not deserving of a death sentence. Policy makers would do well to remember that dysfunctional IDUs will behave as they do until or unless treatment and education can reach them. Rather than placing the user in the crosshairs of punishment, a drug policy focusing on education to prevent abuse, and treatment to minimize the harm of drugs, would help to reduce rather than increase this pitiable group.

## Treatment of IDUs and the Prevention of AIDS

As previously stated, the vast majority of IDUs are heroin addicts. By far the most common treatment for heroin addiction is methadone maintenance. Critics claim that methadone simply substitutes one addiction for another, but it does have several advantages over heroin addiction. Because a methadone high is less euphoric than heroin, methadone addiction is easier to break. A clinical dose lasts from 24 to 36 hours and allows the user to function almost normally, thus making meaningful employment possible. Because it is taken orally, it breaks the ritual cycle of injection, thus reducing needle sharing and the spread of HIV. As many as 100,000 addicts in the United States receive methadone maintenance.[41]

Dr. Robert Newman, head of New York's Beth Israel Medical Center, the largest treatment network in the country, noting the acute shortage of methadone treatment slots, observes: "In essence we have 200,000 heroin addicts in New York and 33,000 methadone maintenance slots, all of which are always filled. These are people who are killing themselves and who are a plague on the rest of us. Out of our own self-interest, voting, tax-paying, drug-free Americans ought to provide more treatment."[42]

Realistically, Dr. Newman's call for more treatment capacity can only be answered if major new funding sources can be tapped. Harnessing the vast cash-generating power of drug sales to this task can only be done if the money that now flows to the coffers of the cartels can be redirected into funding harm reduction programs.

# 10

<hr />

# THE FUTILITY OF INTERDICTION

### The Open Borders of a Free Society

A free and open society is immeasurably more susceptible to drug traffickers than societies with less liberty. The United States is not only a nation whose borders, both internal and external, can be readily crossed but also is the world's richest illicit-drug market. To the east and west are open ocean, to the north the world's longest unfortified border (over 3,000 miles) with Canada, and to the south, a combination of water and a largely desolate, vulnerable border with Mexico punctuated by porous border cities like El Paso and San Diego. This openness makes effective drug supply interdiction impossible.

The United States has spared neither money nor muscle in its efforts to staunch the flow of illicit drugs. Yet drugs are just as available today as they were in 1969, when President Nixon kicked off his war on drugs by ordering the inspection of every vehicle crossing from Mexico into the United States. On the first day 100,000 cars were searched but no drugs were found. The traffic jams were monumental, as was the frustration. After 21 days of chaos at the border, Operation Intercept was mercifully canceled, the first of many failed attempts to seal our southern border against drug traffic. Today, the standard for border crossings is to clear a car every 30 seconds, hardly a time interval to allow real scrutiny.

The U.S. Border Patrol between the United States and Mexico makes more arrests than any other U.S. law enforcement agency, according to the Immigration and Naturalization Service. Most arrests are for unlawful entry into the United States, but a substantial portion are for drug smuggling. From 1982 to 1992 the ranks of Border Patrol agents grew from 2,227 to 4,002, of which 92 percent are deployed along our southern borders and ports, where the third world collides with the first. Only 8 percent are stationed on our much longer northern border with Canada. If the United States decided to seal its southern border against drug inflow, smugglers would simply reroute their cargo to the north.

## A Really Close Family

In February 1993, PBS's "Frontline" show, "What Happened to the Drug War?" told of the Tapia family of El Paso that used a fleet of five luxury sedans with commodious trunks to transport Colombian cocaine across the border from Juarez, Mexico. Each night the family would drive one to five loads from Juarez to a warehouse in El Paso. Over a period of 18 months, more than 900 carloads made it through customs without a single loss. From the El Paso warehouse, trucks laden with cargoes of cocaine hidden within a shipment of Mexican curios would take circuitous routes to Los Angeles. At one particularly dangerous checkpoint, several cars equipped with cellular phones went through ahead of the trucks to insure that no drug-sniffing dogs or other unusual threats were present.

The luck of the drug-smuggling Tapias finally ran out when a tip resulted in the largest cocaine bust in our country's history at that time — 22 tons plus bags of currency totaling more than $12 million. Seized records showed that the family had brought in more than 250 tons of Colombian cocaine. The bookkeeper for the organization testified under oath that $10,000 per load had been paid to unnamed customs inspectors.[1] Customs officials insist that their investigation turned up no such illicit activity, but questions persist about how so much cocaine could be moved through the same gateway for so long without detection.

## One If By Land, Two If By Sea

A sobering fact is that El Paso is only one of 28 gateways into the United States along the Mexican border. As large as the Tapia bust was, there was no perceptible drop in the availability of cocaine on American streets thereafter, nor was there the increase in price that would indicate a decrease in supply.

In addition to the entry points from Mexico and Canada, the thousands of miles of coastline of the Atlantic, the Pacific, and the Gulf of Mexico provide a myriad of unguarded points of access to our lucrative drug markets. Up until the mid-eighties, small, high-speed boats operated out of southern Florida or Texas were used by drug traffickers to pick up waterproofed bundles of marijuana or cocaine dropped from airplanes or transferred from small freighters coming from South or Central American ports. To counter this activity, the Customs Service acquired a fleet of 130 "go-fast" boats at a cost to the taxpayers of $150,000 each. But no sooner were they deployed than the smugglers changed their methods. One customs inspector who was assigned to this operation said that during the five years he ran one of these boats he did not intercept a single small boat carrying drugs. Another agent, a four-year veteran, characterized his efforts as fishing and "burning holes in the water," again without a single drug bust to his craft's credit. The program was finally scuttled in 1991.

Experienced drug enforcement agents agree that drug traffickers are getting smarter and more difficult to combat. Dealers with weak and inept organizations are weeded out and replaced by those who operate more efficiently. This natural selection process helps explain the continued success of the cartels and other drug-selling organizations, in spite of ever-increasing manpower and money expended against them.

The most important tests of the effectiveness of interdiction are the price and availability of drugs. According to figures released in

November 1997 by the Office of National Drug Control Policy, prices of cocaine dropped from $177 per pure gram in 1988 to $139 in 1995. The basic law of supply and demand dictates that if interdiction were effective, the price would have risen. The report did contain some good news, however: estimated cocaine shipments to the United States in 1995 were from 421 to 513 metric tons. That was a drop from the 1989 figure of 547 to 660 metric tons. Seizures also dropped, from 115 tons in 1989 to 98 tons in 1995, demonstrating that the reduction in cocaine shipments was the result of lower demand rather than more effective interdiction.[2] In August 1993, the ONDCP reported an alarming drop in price and an increase in purity of heroin in the United States. Its data "show a clear trend toward lower unit prices and higher purity."[3]

Looking at the issue of availability is also disturbing. A study of out-of-school youths revealed a startling comparison between the availability of alcohol and drugs. It wasn't too surprising that nearly 80 percent said alcohol was "fairly" or "very" easy to obtain — but 82.6 percent said the same of drugs.[4] When a segment of our population perceives the availability of drugs to be even greater than alcohol, it speaks volumes on the failure of interdiction.

## No Fear of Flying

A visible example of wasting taxpayer's money in the pursuit of drug interdiction is the attempted use of radar-bearing balloons, called aerostats, to spot incoming drug-smuggling aircraft and other illegal border crossings, and to alert airborne interceptors. Originally, 9 of these $18 million, flying white elephants were deployed along the border with Mexico. By 1997 the fleet had grown to 11 aerostats with an annual operating budget of $34 million. Designed for unmanned flight at altitudes of 10,000 to 12,000 feet at the end of a tether attached to the ground, they have several operational problems that make them ineffective. The most serious and obvious is that the balloons must be lowered to the ground in high winds. If not, they break up and crash, and million-dollar repair bills are not uncommon. During 1992, the official work log showed that the aerostats were airborne an average of 39.9 percent of the time. Aware of this weakness, smugglers simply wait for foul weather or other operational problems, and then fly their illicit loads with impunity.

Even when the aerostats are aloft they are vulnerable. Several areas, such as the Baboquivari range, south of the aerostat at Fort Huachuca, Arizona, can be penetrated simply by putting a mountain between smugglers' airplanes and the aerostat's line of sight. Since radar does not have the ability to see through rock, smugglers can evade the aerostat's radar by flying lower than the mountain's profile, sometimes as low as 30 feet. Dangerous work, but drug smugglers making hundreds of thousands of dollars from a load of cocaine or heroin are willing to take chances.

A story is told of a smuggler-pilot who was approached by two drug dealers from Mexico at an air strip outside El Paso. They told him they had an airplane and would pay him $15,000 to fly it into Mexico, pick up a load of dope, and fly back to El Paso. The pilot carefully calculated the distance, the weight of the load and the range of the airplane's fuel capacity, and determined that the plane would not make it without stopping to refuel. The drug dealers insisted that refueling was out of the question, saying that the time required would queer the deal. They then raised their offer to $20,000. The pilot reminded them that the airplane flew on fuel, not on money; it simply wouldn't make it. At this the dealers raised their price to $25,000. Exasperated, the pilot started to walk away and they said, "We'll throw in the airplane!" A risk taker, like all smugglers, he accepted their offer. He ended up crash-landing in the Mexican desert and hitchhiking back to the border. He said, "I knew I wasn't going to make it back, but hell, once they threw in the airplane, I just couldn't pass it up. It was worth the gamble."[5]

An even more grandiose example of the willingness of drug smugglers to spend vast amounts of money plying their trade is their recent discovery of old passenger jets as smuggling vehicles. Some of the growing fleet of retired Boeing 727s and similar passenger jets are being bought up at bargain-basement prices and pressed into service to fly drug loads from Colombia to Mexico, Canada, Portugal, and West Africa for eventual sale in the United States and Europe. These planes can outrun the piston-driven, antidrug aircraft currently deployed by the United States and Mexico. Some of the big jets are modified to fly up to 8,000 miles without refueling and can carry loads of up to 22 tons of drugs. A load that size has a street value of $1.8 billion — or the annual gross domestic product of Barbados.[6]

## Inventive Drug Smuggling

The DEA produces a report, which it shares with other drug law enforcement groups, that lists the latest concealment methods it has encountered. The report shows that woodworking and drug smuggling go hand in hand. In New York some years ago, more than 30 pounds of opium sticks were found in the hollowed-out backing of picture frames from Iran. The pictures were of no less a personage than the Ayatollah Khomeini. From Thailand came some beautifully crafted wooden room dividers complete with hidden compartments containing 8 pounds of heroin. Lebanon sent some wooden gaming tables with matching oil lamps. The game boards cleverly concealed 260 pounds of hashish, while the lamps were filled with 15 pounds of hashish oil.[7]

From San Francisco came a report of cocaine being formed into automotive gaskets, floor tiles, children's car seats, and intricately crafted Nativity scenes. A gray, hard-sided, realistic looking suitcase with sides made of a cocaine-plastic mix can hide as much as 13 pounds of cocaine with a street value up to $48,000. Some of these permutations are part of the personal experience of Mike Fleming, a U.S. Customs Service spokesman for the Pacific Region. "The imagination is the limitation," he said. "The next thing you know, they'll make a 747 out of cocaine and fly it into Los Angeles Airport."

In northeastern Canada, on the island of Newfoundland, lies a town with the lyrical name of Little Heart's Ease. This is codfishing country. The trouble is, the cod are so few in number now that the local fisherman have been tempted to engage in other pursuits, one of which is drug smuggling. The holds of sturdy codfishing boats are perfect for gummy slabs of hashish resin pressed into what look like shoe soles. One such seaworthy trawler, *Le Quidam Gaspé*, captained by a former codfisherman, rendezvoused with an incoming freighter from Asia outside the 200-mile limit and took on a cargo of hashish. It then returned to Little Heart's Ease, where the captain planned to secrete its cargo in a waiting truck. Unfortunately for the fisherman, the Royal Canadian Mounties were waiting for him and his 25 tons of hashish, with a street value pegged at $500 million, the largest bust in Newfoundland history.[8]

Couriers or "mules," masquerading as airline passengers frequently swallow condoms full of cocaine or heroin. They are virtually unstoppable, and can bring in a pound or two with a street value of $100,000 or more. The method is favored by many small-time operators, but it poses grave danger to the mule. If a condom containing cocaine breaks in the digestive tract, the mule is dead in a matter of seconds. If the condom contains heroin, he or she could survive for as long as two hours.[9]

Heroin covered with a protective coating and then ingested by poor Colombian farm workers is a variation on the same theme. Heroin is favored for this technique because it is more compact than cocaine and sells for about $100,000 per pound, of which the mule usually gets a 5 percent cut. Stopped at Miami International Airport because they looked nervous and out of place, a mother and her two teenage children from Barranquilla, Colombia, were sent to the hospital and X-rayed. The pictures revealed that they were full of heroin pellets. The family was presented with doses of a strong laxative and rubber gloves. They were then made to pick more than 200 pellets from their own excrement.[10]

## The Militarization of Interdiction

When tottering, often despotic, regimes to our south make a case that the insurgent opposition is rife with drug merchants, our zeal to prosecute the war on drugs produces money, equipment, arms, and in some cases men to fight the good fight. As far back as 1974, when Juan Perón returned from exile to govern Argentina again, he used drugs as a pretext for asking the United States for counterinsurgency help. The United States helped train, equip, and finance a group supposedly intended to combat the drug trade but that later was used by Perón and his police commissioner, José Lopez Rega, as a virtual death squad. Lopez Rega was later found guilty of both murder and drug trafficking.

Since this idea of gaining U.S. support against insurgents by playing the antidrug card was first introduced by Perón and Lopez Rega, many other military regimes throughout South and Central America have used the ploy.

The 1994 invasion of Haiti by the United States to allow the democratically elected Jean-Bertrand Aristide to take over the government from the military was justified by the claim that the Haitian military was heavily involved in drug trafficking, and the flow of drugs from Haiti to the United States constituted a threat to our country. Yet prior to the invasion, during the fiscal year that ended September 30, 1993, Haiti ranked eighth out of ten South and Central American countries originating drug shipments seized in south Florida. Colombia was first with 37,000 pounds seized, Panama was second with 14,000 pounds, and Venezuela third at 8,500 pounds. Eighth-placed Haiti was the shipping point for 1,000 pounds, hardly an amount to qualify them for invasion.[11]

Easily the most egregious example of heavy-handed American foreign policy in the name of the drug war was the invasion of Panama for the single purpose of arresting its drug-dealing president, Manuel Noriega. The invasion, which resulted in the deaths of 300 to 400 (the exact number is still unconfirmed) Panamanian soldiers and civilians, as well as 23 American soldiers and sailors who participated, was justifiable neither by precedent, objective, nor outcome.[12] Noriega had been secretly on the U.S. payroll since 1967 to help fight the spread of communism in Central and South America. In the process, he was co-opted by drug traffickers anxious to utilize Panama's strategic location and lax banking laws to ship their drugs and launder their lucre. With the winding down of the Cold War, Noriega's dual roles as drug-trade facilitator and president of Panama became intolerable to the Bush administration, and the decision was made to invade. There is no doubt that Noriega deserved to be arrested, tried, and convicted, and he is now serving a 40-year term in our federal prison system.

From the Latin American perspective, here is the view: The United States, that colossus from the north, invaded a tiny but sovereign Latin American nation, doing great physical damage to that nation and in the process killing and wounding hundreds of its citizens, all for the purpose of taking one man into custody for trial in its own courts. Noriega's crime: enriching himself by aiding and abetting the sale and shipment of substances to the invader's country, which are in great demand there. The result: Guillermo Endara, the new president installed by the United States, was widely reported to have strong connections to the drug trade himself. Post-invasion Panama is now more active than ever as a center for drug-money laundering. It is a transshipment point for precursor chemicals that are diverted to drug manufacturers in other Latin American countries. In short: Nothing has changed except the names and faces. The flow of drugs and the laundering of illicit cash continue unabated.

The appointment and rapid confirmation of former army general Barry R. McCaffrey in February 1996 to replace Lee P. Brown as the Clinton administration's drug czar demonstrated once again our military mind-set in the drug war. General McCaffrey's appointment promises a tightening of the hold on drug policy by those who would protect the status quo. In spite of the general's distinguished military record, our nation's antidrug efforts would have been better served by the appointment of someone schooled in treatment or education rather than a military man whose point of view almost certainly precludes recognition of the futility of interdiction.

## A Rising Chorus of Criticism

Louis J. Rodrigues, a senior official with the General Accounting Office, in testimony before the Senate Appropriations Subcommittee in February 1993, said:

> *Interdiction has* **not made a difference** *in terms of the higher goals of deterring smugglers and reducing the flow of cocaine. The portion of the federal drug budget allocated to supply reduction initiatives has almost doubled over the last five years, and funding for Department of Defense's detection and monitoring mission has increased over 400% since 1989. Yet cocaine remains affordable, its purity remains high, and it continues to be readily available on American streets (emphasis added).*[13]

Attorney General Janet Reno, addressing the National Summit on Drug Policy the same year, also openly questioned interdiction's effectiveness. She admitted that to put a dent in drug use, interdiction would have to stop at least 75 percent of incoming drugs, an objective she correctly labeled as "economically prohibitive." At the same meeting, Rep. Charles E. Schumer (Democrat, N.Y.), who chaired both the meeting and the House Judiciary Subcommittee on Crime and Criminal Justice, said President Clinton should abolish the interdiction program and called it "a near total failure."[14] He buttressed his argument with estimates that a single 20-square-mile field of opium poppies would produce sufficient heroin for U.S. demand, and that a year's supply of cocaine for the U.S. could be carried in four 747 cargo planes.

## A Summary of the Case Against Interdiction

Jerome H. Skolnick, professor of law at the University of California–Berkeley, in his essay "Rethinking the Drug Problem," sums up the case against interdiction succinctly:

> *Interdiction advocates vastly overestimate the costs that interdiction imposes on drug trafficking. Interdiction is supposed to reduce street sales by increasing smuggling costs — in effect, taxing smuggling — and thus raising the street price. This assumes that smuggling costs constitute a significant percentage of street price. But that simply is not true. It is relatively cheap to produce and refine a kilo of cocaine, perhaps around $1,000 for a kilo that might eventually retail for $250,000 when broken down into quarter- or even eighth-gram units. Smuggling costs might amount to an additional few percent of the retail price. In actuality, most of the retail price of cocaine is divided among those who distribute it on this side of the border. Rand economist Peter Reuter writes, "Fully 99 percent of the price of the drug when sold on the streets of the United States is accounted for by payments to people who distribute it. Thus, if a kilo of cocaine retails for $250,000, smuggling costs account for around $2,500. A doubling or tripling of smuggling costs accordingly has a negligible impact on street price. Combined with the vastly increased production which has driven prices down,* **interdiction has had little, if any, positive effects** *— and these can be outweighed by the unanticipated side effect of strengthening drug marketing organizations" (emphasis added).*[15]

The highest published estimate of the proportion of incoming drugs that are actually stopped at our borders is 25 percent. The mean estimate is 10 percent. Is the United States too stupid or stubborn to admit that the task is impossible? No. The truth is that there are large numbers of people whose jobs, careers, and feelings of accomplishment are tied to the drug interdiction enterprise. For the most part, they are dedicated, honest individuals who do a difficult, often dangerous job. But their mission is impossible.

Should Washington finally decide that the tactic of interdiction is not working, there is every reason to expect that any new tactics within the overall strategy of prohibition will also fail.

# 11

⟁⬥⟁

# THE WORLD IS A PUSHER

## Mexico and Colombia — Our Amigos or Not?

It would be hard to find two countries that share so long a border and so little else as do Mexico and the United States. Separate languages, dissimilar cultures, disparate levels of economic development and different legal systems all serve to make the relationship a difficult one. Furthermore, trying to stop the flow of illegal substances from one country to the other is a recipe for endless antagonism.

Incidents such as the following add to the perception of many U.S. officials and much of the American press that Mexico is not really serious about waging the war on drugs. In 1992 the Mexican federal attorney general's office offered up impressive statistics to show the growth and vigor of its antidrug efforts (a combined 70,000 acres of marijuana and opium (heroin) poppies destroyed, plus seizures by Mexican authorities of marijuana, cocaine, and heroin totaling 880,200 pounds). But critics point to the questionable reputation of Mexican government statistics, which outrages Mexican nationals, and fuels further skepticism north of the border. Neither reaction promotes healthy foreign relations.

The brutal 1985 torture and murder by Mexican drug dealers of an American DEA agent, Enrique "Ricky" Camarena, on assignment in Mexico at the time of his death, set off a chain of international events that have been chronicled by journalists and moviemakers. The dealers responsible for Camarena's death made the mistake of victimizing a man respected by loyal colleagues who vowed to avenge his murder. Dr. Humberto Alvarez Machain, who Camarena's friends thought had been the medical mind keeping Camarena alive during what the autopsy showed to be grisly torture, eluded the avengers. Nearly five years after his death, Camarena's DEA friends hired a bounty hunter to kidnap Dr. Machain in Mexico and smuggle him to Los Angeles and jail. President Carlos Salinas de Gortari and the Mexican people considered this an insult to the sovereignty of Mexico. Eventually Dr. Machain was released and flown back to Mexico. An agreement was subsequently struck to prohibit either country from abducting suspects from the other's territory.

Also damaging to Mexico's image was the 1993 killing of Roman Catholic cardinal Posadas Ocampo in the parking lot of the airport at Guadalajara. The prelate died, along with his driver and five other people, in what the Mexican government called a case of mistaken identity. The alleged intended victim, a notorious drug trafficker named Joaquin Guzman, escaped unharmed. The official explanation was that the cardinal's fatal error was driving to the airport in a white Mercury limousine with tinted windows, a vehicle favored by drug traffickers like Guzman. But other factors remained unexplained. Why did an Aeromexico flight wait patiently on the tarmac for 20 minutes after its scheduled departure, allowing members of the Tijuana cartel participating in the shooting to board the plane to Tijuana, where they deplaned and disappeared?[1] Nor was it explained why the cardinal, clad in clerical robes, was shot over a dozen times at close range. Cardinal Posadas' successor, Juan Sandoval, says he has four witnesses who insist that the killing was not accidental.[2]

Echoing the sentiments of many people on both sides of the border, Eduardo Valle Espinoza, a top aide to Mexico's attorney general, asked in his letter of resignation, "When are we going to have the courage and political maturity to tell the Mexican people that we suffer from a sort of narco-democracy?"[3] These are not reassuring words from our neighbor to the south with whom we share that long and vulnerable border. Latest figures show that 70 percent of the cocaine consumed in the U.S. now comes across that border.

## Colombia: Good and Evil

Located on the northwestern coast of South America, where the umbilical cord called Panama connects Central America to the South American continent, Colombia is both strategically located and topographically perfect as an ideal cocaine source for the United States. This accident of geography is enhanced by the presence of a large poverty-stricken population in both the mountainous rural areas and the urban slums of Bogotá, Medellín, and Cali, providing thousands of people whose desperation to feed their families often makes them willing participants in the drug trade. It is estimated that 80 percent of the cocaine consumed in the United States is manufactured in Colombia.[4]

From the Colombian citizen's perspective, cocaine is a problem, but far from their largest. True, since the 1994 Colombian presidential election there has been an ongoing debate about drug money as a possible source of campaign funds. But during the actual campaign, cocaine trafficking was a minor issue, as debate centered on jobs, education, poverty relief, and years of conflict with leftist guerrillas, many of whom are avowed Marxists. These revolutionaries control 40 percent of the nation's territory, mostly in sparsely populated regions.

Two men, one famous and the other infamous, are microcosms of the Colombian drug conundrum. Dr. Gustavo de Greiff was the country's heroic prosecutor general from 1991 until his mandatory retirement at age 65 in 1994. His is a story of courage in the face of danger and political attack. The other man, Pablo Escobar, was the richest, most murderous outlaw of his time.

Prosecutor General de Greiff was the equivalent of our attorney general. Merely by accepting that job in a country where high-level corruption is so common and drug war violence so vicious, he showed himself to be a man of extraordinary courage. In a country where both prosecutors and judges must wear disguises in court to avoid being targets for drug dealers outside the court, one can only imagine the kind of danger faced by Dr. de Greiff. Colombia has a current rate of 70 murders per 100,000 people (the U.S. has an annual homicide rate of 11 murders per 100,000). Medellín alone suffers a sickening murder rate of 250 per 100,000 population.[5] Among Dr. de Greiff's many accomplishments while he was in office was the elimination of Pablo Escobar and his Medellín cartel. Also, the conviction rate for drug dealers rose from 20 percent to 75 percent.[6]

Dr. de Greiff and his family lived in Bogotá in what amounted to a bunker. He rode to and from his house in a bomb- and bullet-proof car. His street was closed to traffic to protect him from attack by drug dealers. His wife, two daughters, and grandchildren had to leave Colombia at various times because of threats on their lives. A national icon in Colombia, where his retirement was regretted by nearly all informed Colombians, Dr. de Greiff was vilified while in office by U.S. Senator John Kerry (Democrat, Mass.) and U.S. Attorney General Janet Reno. In a statement Senator Kerry said, "His [de Greiff's] positions are nearly identical with those of the cartel itself. As such, they demonstrate the degree to which the Cali cartel has already gained influence in the very offices of Colombian law enforcement that are supposed to protect society against the Cartel." The senator later denied that his words questioned Dr. de Greiff's integrity.

Not only did Senator Kerry's criticism amount to second-guessing of the efforts of a sovereign nation to solve a domestic problem, he further demonstrated his lack of understanding of the Colombian situation by adding, "Of course the cartels want it [legalization]. Instead of Juan Valdez picking coffee, you'll have Juan Valdez promoting the best coca leaf."[7]

U.S. Attorney General Reno showed an equal failure to grasp the realities of the drug war and the effect it has on foreign relations. After several years in the trenches of the drug war, Dr. de Greiff had announced his opinion that legalization of drugs in Colombia was the only way to deprive the cartels of their massive drug profits. Put off by Dr. de Greiff's comments, Attorney General Reno decided that the United States should no longer cooperate with Colombia in sharing evidence for prosecuting drug dealers. This was a self-defeating strategy as well as an insult to Colombia and was soon rescinded.

Contrary to Senator Kerry's and Attorney General Reno's opinions, legalization is the worst thing that could happen to the cartels. With legalization, the supply of cocaine would come from legitimate, controlled sources at controlled prices, not at the hugely inflated prices that now fill the cartels' coffers. With wisely imple-mented legalization, the drug cartels would cease to exist.

## The Saga of Pablo Escobar

Pablo Escobar, the head of the Medellín cartel, seemed impervious to law and order during the decade from the early 1980s until his death in 1993. In 1982, at the age of 27, he was an established drug smuggler with a growing fleet of airplanes. He ultimately controlled 60 percent of Colombia's cocaine, which was 80 percent of the U.S. supply. Escobar bribed, murdered, and terrorized without remorse.

In 1982, having already amassed a fortune without being gener-ally recognized as an outlaw, Escobar successfully ran for Congress as an alternative representative from Medellin's state, Antioquia. He could fill in for the regular member in his absence; more important, the office carried with it legal immunity. Two years later, Escobar lost his congressional seat when his criminal record was revealed by a courageous justice minister, Rodrigo Lara Bonilla, who later paid for his courage with his life. Escobar was reportedly linked to his murder.[8]

At one point in his murderous career, Escobar offered a bounty on policemen, paying $2,100 for each officer killed. Over 300 police-men died as a result.[9]

In its July 7, 1988 issue, *Forbes* magazine listed Escobar as one of the world's richest men, showing his net worth as $2.5 billion. Conspicuous as a philanthropist, Escobar had donated soccer stadiums, roller rinks, road paving, and housing projects for poor Colombians. Unconcerned that the money was tainted and the donor a killer, many citizens mourned him at his funeral, after he died in a hail of bullets from an elite force of police and soldiers on December 2, 1993, the day after his 44th birthday.

Informed observers predicted that Escobar's demise would not change the Colombian drug trade. Their predictions proved accurate; the Cali cartel was only too happy to take up the slack. Only the names and faces of the players changed.

## There's an Awful Lot of Coca in Peru (and Bolivia, Too)

Peru was the source of 49 percent of the world's hardy, fast-growing coca leaf — about 130,200 metric tons of leaves in 1997.[10] It is a favorite of the poor Peruvian farmer because it pays more than other crops. That a vast majority of their production ends up as cocaine is a vague, legal abstraction to the Peruvian farmers, since for centuries, residents of the rugged Andes mountains have chewed coca leaf for medicine and pleasure. Peru derives 2.4 times the income from coca than it does from cocoa,[11] a distant second in cash value. A peasant leader near the rural town of Soritor said, "Our problems are economic, and the answer to survival is to go to coca."[12] It is no surprise that Peru's government has not been successful in stamping out coca production. In addition, the Maoist Sendero Luminoso (Shining Path) guerrillas, who reportedly control one fifth of the country, often assist both farmers and drug dealers in resisting the efforts of Peruvian and U.S. coca eradication and interdiction operations, thus befriending the farmers while swelling the ranks of Sendero's guerrilla movement.

President Alberto Fujimori of Peru, who won notoriety for his tough handling of the 1997 rebel takeover of the Japanese consulate in Lima, has proclaimed, "Put it in the headlines, the world's antidrug strategy is a failure." On another occasion, when being interviewed by the Peruvian newspaper *La Republica*, he said, "The social cost of a war on drugs with strict application of the law would be terrible, because it would involve jailing 200,000 farmers.[13]

According to estimates, Bolivia produces about 26 percent of the world's coca leaf.[14] Lying immediately southeast of Peru, it has similar topography and climate. There is some cocaine production within the country, but most of its coca leaf is exported. The second-poorest nation in the hemisphere after Haiti, Bolivia finds the high dollar yield per acre nearly irresistible. Yet there appears to be a concerted effort by the government to combat drug trafficking. Figures released in 1993 by the Bolivian Interior Ministry showed that 35 percent of the growing prison population was incarcerated for drug-related offenses. In 1995 and 1996, leaf production was reduced due to the government's eradication efforts.[15]

Colombia, Peru, and Bolivia produce an estimated 95 percent of the world's coca.[16] Some drug warriors have suggested that the way to fight the drug war from the supply side is to destroy, not the plants themselves, but the drug labs, or "kitchens," which make the stuff. The DEA and the State Department launched joint efforts with several South American countries as long ago as 1987, aimed at destroying drug labs. In one nine-month period, some 1,375 labs were dismantled throughout South and Central America.[17] In spite of the impressive success of "Operation White Cap," there was no change in the availability or price of cocaine. Destroying labs that produce a valuable finished product can only cause them to reappear in other jungle enclaves or mountain hideaways or on some other continent, where greed, hunger, and a suitable climate coincide.

## Europe's Involvement

In June 1993, Lisbon hosted the first International Conference on Cocaine Trafficking and Organized Crime. At the conference,

Interpol Secretary-General Raymond Kendall warned that the opening of borders, resulting from both the breakup of the Soviet Union and the formation of the European Community, has resulted in a fresh surge of drug trafficking and organized crime. Another speaker at the conference, Portugal's justice minister, Laborinho Lucio, acknowledged that his country was being used as a "springboard into the rest of Europe" for drug shipments. He should have added, ". . . and from there into the United States as well."

Elsewhere in Europe, the Balkan countries, when they are not too busy fighting wars, are actively smuggling heroin. Alain Labrousse, the director of a Paris-based research organization that monitors global drug trafficking, said:

> *Albanians have enlisted assistance from Serbs . . . along the Kosovo frontier to help with their smuggling operations. It reminds me of the Lebanese civil war, when Shiites and Sunnis and Maronites were all fighting each other, but continued to cooperate in drug traffic. It shows again that money is more important than war and ethnic hatred.*[18]

Opportunities created by the breakup of the former Soviet Union did not escape the notice of the Mafia. *Newsweek,* in its December 13, 1993, issue, devoted a "Special Report" to what it called "The Global Mafia." In the report, Roy Godson, of Washington's National Strategy Information Center, estimated organized crime's annual worldwide profits at $1 trillion. A substantial percentage of that money was made in the drug business. Gone are the *Godfather* days when the Mafia was portrayed as considering drugs to be "too dirty" for their hands.

Responding to this reality, Italy and Russia signed an accord in Moscow on September 11, 1993, to insure cooperation between the two nations in combating organized crime, money laundering and drug trafficking.

## Asia and the Golden Triangle

Heroin is the drug growth stock of the 1990s. The United States, which until recently consumed about 6 percent of the world's heroin (compared to 60 percent of all illicit drugs), is looked at lustfully by the heroin sellers of the world as an enormous growth market. An estimated 75 percent of the world's opium poppies are grown in the three countries comprising the Golden Triangle, Burma (now Myanmar), Thailand and Laos. They produce about 2,800 tons of raw opium per year. Pakistan and Afghanistan contribute another 870 tons to the total.[19] During a 1994 visit to the area, former American drug czar Lee P. Brown was advised that the only way to make any progress in fighting the heroin flow from Asia was to work through Myanmar, by far the largest producer and the dominant member of the triumvirate.

Nigeria, located over 3,000 miles away on the west coast of Africa, is an unlikely ally of the Golden Triangle countries. It is favored because of its long experience in drug smuggling, as a trans-shipment center, and its connections with American and European drug dealers. Current estimates are that 35 to 40 percent of all heroin entering the United States comes through Nigeria.[20] In April 1994, President Clinton added Nigeria to the list of pariah countries such as Iran, Syria, and Myanmar) that receive no American non-humanitarian aid. Unfortunately, this move has not diminished the flow of drugs from Nigeria into the United States.

## Afghanistan: Long-Term Instability

When the Russians finally withdrew their support for the government of Afghanistan after the collapse of the Soviet Union, they left behind in that country what a Pakistani intelligence official called a 10-year stock of arms and ammunition, plus fleets of tanks, armored vehicles and helicopters.[21] With the country's small agricultural and industrial base in ruins, Afghans turned to selling either drugs or guns. A worker in the Katchi Garhi refugee camp in Pakistan said in 1993 of the 30,000 refugees who had recently left the camp, "Most will plant poppies. When I go back, I will too. What else can I do? I am a teacher, but there are no schools. No factories. No work. No irrigation. How can we eat?" This harsh reality led to an increase in Afghan opium production from 200 tons per year in 1971 to 2800 tons in 1996.[22]

## Conclusions

From this brief tour of the world — by no means all-inclusive — one can see that the sources of drugs are many and varied. Each major illicit drug — heroin, cocaine, marijuana, and its derivative, hashish — has several sources already in place and others waiting in the wings. Because of the enormous profits produced, stopping the flow of a particular drug from one source merely causes another immediately to take its place.

Implicit in the entire interdiction enterprise is the notion that if the United States could only stop foreign countries from producing illicit drugs, we could solve the drug problem at home. Nothing could be further from the truth. The problem lies squarely at our own feet.

Jeane Kirkpatrick, the former U.S. ambassador to the United Nations, put it this way:

> *Drug production is not the problem. Consumption is the problem. Even if we were able to cut off all importation of foreign produced drugs, we would not solve the problem. . . . [T]he problem is fundamentally a domestic one. Obviously the U.S. government can hardly hold others responsible for a failure to control problems that we cannot control in our own nation's capital.*[23]

In 1997 the federal government spent $1.4 billion on interdiction, with little if any tangible impact on the problem.[24] If that money had been spent on antidrug education and treatment, not only would Americans have received real value for their tax dollars, but also many would enjoy a much-improved quality of life.

# 12

---

# REDUCING SOCIETAL DAMAGE WITH A DIFFERENT DRUG STRATEGY

An ancient Turkish proverb warns, "When you tell the truth, have one foot in the stirrup." American drug policy critics need both feet in the stirrups as they struggle to convey two profound truths to our country's drug warriors:

1. The demand for mind-altering substances has been a part of mankind since its beginning. No amount of wishing or well-intentioned legislation will eliminate that demand.

2. As long as there is this demand, even though these substances remain illegal, the marketplace will continue to supply them.

Since the 1914 passage of the Harrison Narcotics Act, designed primarily to bring state-to-state consistency to our illicit drug laws, the United States has spent billions of dollars trying to stifle the demand for illegal drugs. Our main thrust in demand reduction has been to pass increasingly harsh laws to punish those who consume the forbidden fruit, relying on coercion rather than reason. Meanwhile, our efforts to cut off the supply of illicit drugs have been as futile as they have been expensive. Every resource available to the world's richest nation has not prevented the flow of drugs into the U.S.

From many quarters comes the indictment that our antidrug policy is a failure. Attorney General Janet Reno has publicly declared the two main elements of the strategy, interdiction and the jailing of drug offenders, to be failures.[1]

The Association of the Bar of the City of New York appointed a committee to study the wisdom of current drug laws. After an exhaustive study over a period of some seven years, the committee concluded in 1994: "The costs of drug prohibition are simply too high and its benefits too dubious."[2] A recent opinion poll revealed that 70 percent of Americans think the drug war is a failure.

## Bilateral Harm Reduction

Instead of the public will remaining the public "won't", our society could do an unusual and original thing: It could acknowledge that many citizens of the world use and will continue to use mind-altering substances and that as long as they harm no one else, they have a right to do so. This acknowledgment would lead us to replace prohibition with bilateral harm reduction as the centerpiece of America's drug policy. This approach to the drug problem recognizes that both individuals and society are harmed by drugs. It posits that both must benefit simultaneously for a drug policy to be beneficial to either. For example, criminalizing the use of drugs may benefit society in the short run, but it harms incarcerated individuals as well as society in the long run. One of the objectives of bilateral harm reduction is to reduce drug abuse through education. This helps both individuals, by preventing problematic drug use, and society, by reducing crime and the prison population. A basic tenet of bilateral harm reduction is legalization, to eliminate the huge profits from drug dealing and redirect that money into antidrug education, treatment, and research.

Before bilateral harm reduction has any chance of being adopted as the balance wheel of our nation's drug policy, our government must adopt a new mind-set about drugs. As Dr. Ronald Hamowy puts it in the introduction to his book *Dealing with Drugs:*

*There is a certain fanciful quality to the rationale of most government action (and far too many discussions) concerning illicit drugs, that only two possibilities exist, either total abstinence enforced by the police power of the state or uncontrolled use leading to addiction. Drug enforcement agencies have done everything in their power to promote this notion and the media, taking their cue from the government, have bombarded us with this view of drug use.*[3]

Crime and criminals generated by dealers and users in pursuit of profits and money to buy drugs, corruption generated by the sale of illegal drugs leading to a lack of respect for law and order, racial tension and the spread of AIDS — all would be resolved or considerably eased under bilateral harm reduction. Two sources of harm may remain unresolved: the perception by many that inebriating drugs are an affront to morality and the negative impact on society of drug-dependent, nonproductive citizens. The morality issue should be eased somewhat by the knowledge that the removal of drug trafficking as an illegal employment option would save many lives. As for the negative impact of the user's drug dependence or addiction, this will persist always and forever, regardless of the legal status of drugs.

A far superior approach in our drug policy would be a massive strategy of education and treatment — *prevention* rather than *punishment* — to decrease demand for mind-altering substances. The imbalance between punishment and prevention in our current drug policy is evident in the relative funding of the two approaches. Combined state, local, and federal spending on all aspects of the drug war in the mid-1990s exceeded $30 billion per year; about 70 percent to law enforcement and incarceration and only 30 percent to education and treatment.[4] This ratio was improved with 1997 budget requests to about 34 percent for education and treatment,[5] but until the ratios are reversed to favor these vital areas, we are headed in the wrong direction.

## Avoiding Balkanization

There has been considerable experimentation with decriminalization of drugs, particularly in Europe, but there are no unqualified success stories to relate. The main reason is either experience with, or fear of, "balkanization" of the drug problem. If an individual city, region, or country tries to decriminalize drugs, it becomes a magnet for drug users from surrounding jurisdictions with punitive drug laws. Also, with the exception of the Netherlands, which has legalized marijuana, no country has taken the black market's profit out of drugs. Yet profit is the powerful engine that drives the problem.

The classic example of balkanization of drug laws took place in Platzpitz Park in the beautiful lakeside city of Zurich, Switzerland. Zurich attracted drug users from all over Europe because of its lax enforcement of Swiss drug laws. Drugs were sold and used publicly, free of law enforcement, in the park, and soon the scene became so chaotic and menacing that the authorities had to close it down. According to Giorgio Prestele, a drug policy spokesman, 80 percent of the users rounded up were not from Zurich. Platzpitz Park was a failed experiment in drug policy reform because Zurich allowed both drug injection in a public park and public drug intoxication. The United States can learn from this experience.

## No Profits from Drugs

Drug policy reformers are by no means united behind the best way to help the United States extract itself from prohibition. Reformers who endorse decriminalization with no offsetting social benefits loose the immense power of the profit motive. This approach would result in damage to society similar to that now inflicted by alcohol and tobacco. Similarly, the unfettered availability of drugs in millions of outlets throughout the land would dangerously and unnecessarily add to their use.

The profit motive, which has served us so magnificently in our economic development, needs to be reined in when selling products that have clear and present dangers. To insure that the legalization component of harm reduction does not lead to greater use of drugs, *the profit motive must be eliminated entirely from the distribution of drugs.* The means of distribution should lie with the states, in state-controlled retail outlets. Legalized, state-level control and distribution of marijuana, cocaine and heroin, sold at half the retail price now paid to drug dealers, would put the cartels out of business, while, just as importantly, providing necessary funds to support more and better treatment, education, and research programs. Funds that now flow to drug dealers and cartels would instead be diverted to society and then, in a potent irony, turned back against the problem. Drug users would be getting products from FDA-inspected sources, assuring predictable strength and purity. (Nearly all of today's drug-caused deaths are the result of overdoses from drugs of unknown potency or from using harmful substances to dilute the drug.) Adding to the competitive advantage of state-run drug distribution would be the absence of criminality, with its attendant risks and stigmas.

## Preparation [The Nitty Gritty]

Bringing about such sweeping changes in America's drug policy will mean an epic battle in every state. However, as Charles de Gaulle once said, "France was never her true self unless she was engaged in a great enterprise." Casting aside our well-intentioned but failed drug policies and replacing them with bilateral harm reduction through legalization will indeed be "a great enterprise," but it is one of which we are capable.

The keystone of a successful change of national drug policy is preparation. The concept needs to be presold to the public and the state legislatures effectively enough so that we do not endure a period when the nation is a checkerboard of states that have repealed drug prohibition and others that have not. A checkerboard of drug laws would cause states opting for legalization to be inundated by drug users from neighboring states. Only with proper planning and preparation can our nation segue seamlessly from drug prohibition to a policy of bilateral harm reduction.

Checkerboarding could be eliminated by constitutional amendment, but that process would be slow and cumbersome, and the enshrinement of drug legalization in the U.S. Constitution a hard sell. The Twenty-first Amendment was necessary to repeal alcohol prohibition because prohibition had been instituted by the Eighteenth. Drug prohibition was imposed by federal statute and it could be repealed by an act of Congress, a much easier process. The following is a possible scenario: Congress passes legislation whereby individual states can adopt a drug-legalization program. As soon as 35 states have given assurance that they will adopt legalization, the policy change can be implemented by all. With such a strong majority, the balance of the states would soon comply as they witnessed the revenue and quality-of-life advantages accruing to the more progressive states. Alcohol prohibition was repealed in less than a year after Congress proposed it. Why not illegal drugs?

Dr. Arnold S. Trebach, former head of Washington, D.C.'s Drug Policy Foundation, outlined this simple and workable legislative approach to legalization:

> *The major goals of the new laws at the national level would be: first to eliminate the key federal laws imposing criminal penalties on the manufacture, sale and possession of drugs; second to dismantle the Drug Enforcement Administration and assign its staff and functions to the Federal Bureau of Investigation or other federal agencies; third to carve out a new supportive role for the federal government recognizing the primacy of the states in drug control.... As it did in 1933 with alcohol, the federal government would return to the states*

*the primary power to determine which drugs could be legally sold and under what conditions, reversing the direction of most federal drug legislation since early this century.*[6]

The Comprehensive Drug Abuse Prevention and Control Act of 1970, the federal umbrella governing drug control laws, must be repealed.

Two scholars of drug policy, Daniel K. Benjamin and Roger Leroy Miller, coauthors of *Undoing Drugs: Beyond Legalization*, borrowing heavily from the concept and language of the Twenty-first Amendment, have proposed that the following statute be enacted after repeal: "The transportation or importation into any state, territory or possession of the United States for delivery or use therein of any controlled substance, in violation of the laws thereof, is hereby prohibited."[7] The key words there are "in violation of the laws thereof." This phrase refers to the empowerment of the states to make and enforce their own laws concerning drugs.

## State-Controlled Retail Outlets

To distribute drugs at the retail level and remove the profit motive, states could develop controlled outlets similar to those of the 13 states that presently control the retail sale of alchoholic beverages. Alabama serves its approximately 4,000,000 residents with 150 stores. Pennsylvania, the largest state owning its liquor stores, has 680 stores to serve its 12,000,000 people.[8] As with state-controlled liquor stores, a sufficient number of drug outlets would be necessary so that distance would not be a deterrent. The experience of states with their own retail liquor outlets provides encouragement that liquor sales to minors are minimized when alcohol is sold at state-controlled outlets. Milo Kirk, past president of Mothers Against Drunk Driving (MADD), was impressed by the city of Pittsburgh's high rating in a "sting" operation conducted to determine the prevalence of liquor sales to minors: It had the lowest incidence of sales to minors among a number of large cities. Mrs. Kirk said, "Pennsylvania is the largest liquor-control state, and it does a good job of enforcement."[9] If Pennsylvania's positive results with alcohol could be replicated with drugs, the availability of drugs to the underage could be less with legalization than at present.

## Manufacturing and Packaging Legalized Drugs

The dynamics of the free market would determine where drugs were grown, processed and packaged. Whether the source is domestic or foreign, the same strict quality control standards required of today's pharmaceuticals by the Food and Drug Administration would be applied. Packaging of marijuana, cocaine, and heroin sold in state-controlled outlets would be generic in nature and would always contain warning labels similar to those now present on cigarettes. Directions for use would be included, as would addresses and phone numbers for obtaining help with dependence and addiction. Syringes would be included, where appropriate, to make needle sharing unnecessary.

## Pricing Legal Drugs

The twin objectives of drug pricing under legalization would be to price drugs low enough to reduce the profit level so that criminal cartels could no longer compete, but high enough so that the cost is not insignificant to the user. Prices would undoubtedly vary from state to state.

It would be vital to the success of a harm reduction policy that legislation in each state include the provision that profits generated from drug sales could be used *only* to combat drug abuse. There is an appealing self-correcting mechanism in such an approach. If the use of drugs increased in any given state, the funds available to combat the problem would increase because of higher revenue from sales. Conversely, when the problem diminished, revenue would decrease.

This would be in distinct contrast to the usual bureaucracy whose success is measured partly by its ability to obtain ever-increasing funding, regardless of results.

## No Cocaine in Coca-Cola

States must guard against the inclusion of newly legalized drugs as ingredients in commercial products. Until the early 1900s, cocaine was an active, although small, ingredient in Coca-Cola and other widely used products. At the turn of the century, doctors and newspapers took aim at many products containing cocaine and other narcotics, and as a result, many of the products were either altered to exclude the drugs or were later outlawed by our prohibition laws. Today, Coca-Cola contains a "decocainized flavor essence of the coca leaf."[10]

The nonprescription medicine field is particularly prone to the use of stimulants and narcotics as ingredients. This practice is outlawed in most of its harmful forms today, and that limitation should remain in force after legalization.

## The Question of Advertising

Inimical to the objectives of a bilateral harm reduction policy would be any proposal to allow advertising of legalized drugs. Simply put, none would be allowed, nor would there be any sales or marketing activity that would encourage the purchase or use of drugs. Prohibited would be the imaginative, scientifically targeted advertising or promotion such as the character "Joe Camel" and the slogan "This Bud's for You."

The promotion of drug use through movies, television, and song lyrics should continue to be vigorously opposed by public interest groups. The motion picture and television industries have both done an admirable job of minimizing this problem, and their continued responsible behavior would be vital to the success of legalization as a public policy. It can only be hoped that some songwriters (particularly of the rap genre) will mature into their responsibilities as have the other entertainment media.

## Individual Responsibility

None of the foregoing should be interpreted as promoting a culture where irresponsible behavior is either condoned or allowed to go unpunished. Government has a contract with its citizens to enforce the laws in exchange for citizens' agreement to abide by them. No less from either party is acceptable, particularly in a democracy. In a harm reduction paradigm, an integral part of both the education and treatment programs would be to inculcate in our citizenry, young and old, the concept that individual responsibility is the cardinal rule. If you harm another while under the influence of a mind-altering substance, you will be swiftly and surely punished.

Any death caused by drug abuse should be punished as though it were premeditated. Industrial accidents caused by drug abuse should be viewed legally as intentional and punished accordingly. Death from drug overdose should be considered suicide and excluded from life insurance policies. Driving under the influence of drugs should carry the same legal and social sanctions as driving when drunk.

## Financing Education, Treatment, and Research

To propose unfunded public policies in these days of widespread governmental cost-cutting is to invite treatment as an ideological leper. But state sales of legal drugs, even at half the retail prices now paid to drug dealers and the cartels would provide more than adequate funding to support treatment and education programs and research into problematic drug use.

ONDCP's previously mentioned 1997 estimate of spending by Americans for illicit drugs was $57.5 billion. With 1 or 2 percent of that figure going to growers and processors, over $56 billion in gross profit is produced. If legal prices were cut to half of current illegal prices, $28 billion per year would be available to fund the bilateral harm reduction agenda. To be conservative, we will assume a harm reduction budget of $21 billion.

First on the agenda would be treatment on demand for those who have allowed drugs to control their lives. When people are ready to make the effort to turn their lives around, adequate treatment facilities must be available. Because the drug-abusing population is dysfunctional, most will be unable to pay for treatment. Those who can pay all or part of their cost of treatment should. For those who can't pay, treatment should be no less available.

Using the best information available today, the maximum cost of treatment is calculable. About 2,800,000 United States abusers would currently benefit from treatment.[11] If 75 percent took advantage of treatment at an average cost of $5,626 per year, the total annual expenditure would be about $12 billion. (The figure of $5,626 is taken from an analysis by the Rand Corporation that included relatively brief, inexpensive outpatient modalities and long-term residential programs.)

Of our original $21 billion, $9 billion remains in our yearly budget. From it we can fund both an aggressive antidrug education program and research efforts to find a pharmacological answer to addiction and dependence prevention. Addressing first the educational program, we propose that here is the case for a far-reaching, sophisticated advertising campaign, equal to the current combined advertising budgets of the big three automotive companies, General Motors, Ford, and Chrysler, a robust $3.25 billion dollars,[12] to get across the message of the dangerous downside of drugs.[12]

A vital part of bilateral harm reduction is funding agressive research into medical solutions to drug addiction and dependence. As a benchmark, the fiscal 1994 AIDS research budget of the National Institutes of Health was $1.3 billion.[13] Matching that amount by requiring all states to contribute to this vital research fund, would leave a remainder of $4.45 billion to fund the operation of drug outlets in all 50 states.

Balanced federal budget advocates will be happy to learn that no federal monies are anticipated in the execution of the proposed policy. The present federal budget for the drug war is $13 billion per year and rising. Under the bilateral harm reduction approach we would spend over one and a half times that amount with no federal funds required. Not only would this policy do a vastly better job of drug control than the present prohibitionist policies, it would do so at a substantial savings in tax dollars. It is as near perfect as public policies get; the cost of a given problem is paid for by those who are its proximate cause.

## Strong Antidrug Education

In a free society, the best way to mold healthy, informed opinions about any subject is to educate the public and rely on its collective wisdom to draw the appropriate conclusions. Our present attempts at antidrug education programs have met with the limited success commensurate with limited scope and funding. We propose strongly funded programs executed by the 50 states with funds garnered from drug sales in those states. Persuasive examples of what educating the public can accomplish include progress in reducing smoking (down over 38 percent in the last 20 years),[14] the promotion of safety in the workplace (death rate per 100,000 people down 50 percent in the last 30 years),[15] and combating drunk driving (alcohol-related driving deaths down 20 percent in the last two years).[16]

Factual, focused, continuous education can make all the difference with America's youth in their attitude toward drugs, and thus their likelihood of becoming involved. The same can be said of their parents. The Clinton administration's former drug czar, Lee Brown, when asked about reasons for increased drug use among the young, replied: "What is hurting us right now is that the drug issue is not on the radar screen of the media. There's a false perception that drugs are no longer a big problem." Brown went on to cite a study by the Center for Media and Public Affairs that found that television news coverage of the drug problem had dropped from 518 articles in 1989 to just 66 by 1993.[17]

Two present-day drug education programs include the word "resistance" in their titles, recognizing that education to strengthen adolescent resistance to drug use is vital. DARE (Drug Abuse Resistance Education) is a cooperative program between local law enforcement and the schools. While it is not without its critics, it is a national program that forcefully brings an antidrug message from the local police to the schoolchildren of America. Project ALERT (Adolescent Learning Experiences in Resistance Training), a program tested in 30 junior high schools in Oregon and California, is designed to equip students with the social skills that will enable them to resist experimentation with drugs, alcohol and cigarettes.

Such programs hold no guarantee that America's youth will unanimously line up in strict compliance with society's dictates. But neither do they now with prohibitionist policies. In fact, such policies incite adolescents to rebel and experiment. The stronger job we do in committing both funds and resolve to the task of antidrug education, the fewer problematic drug users we will have.

## More Drug Treatment

Recovery from addiction or dependence is not an event but a process. The longer one stays in treatment, the better the chances for a satisfactory outcome. A 1994 study of 12,000 addicts showed that for each month an addict stayed in treatment, the odds of relapse in the following year went down by 6 percent.[18] Last year, Dr. Mitchell Rosenthal, the founder of Phoenix House, claimed a 60 percent success rate among the 70,000 addicted and dependent people he has treated since 1967, most of whom are residents for 12 to 18 months.[19]

In separate studies, the Rand Corporation and the University of Chicago, comparing the cost of source-country control, interdiction, domestic enforcement, and treatment as supply-control techniques, concluded that treatment provided the best return on investment by a wide margin.[20] Rand estimated that "The costs of crime and lost productivity are reduced by $7.46 for every dollar spent on treatment."[21] Most of the treatment payoff came from savings from decreased criminal activity by those treated, as well as fewer hospitalizations and lost productivity.

Today, New York's Beth Israel Medical Center boasts the largest treatment capacity in the country. But waiting lists for a detoxification program there usually run five days to three weeks; waits for methadone maintenance slots may be up to a year.

It is one of the major public policy errors of the war on drugs that so low a percentage of prison inmates with drug problems receive treatment. A 1993 report by Lee Brown stated that each year about 200,000 people with drug-related problems are sent to prison or jail and released without treatment.[22] In some cases, eligibility for parole is used as a carrot to encourage completion of a treatment program while in prison. So why isn't treatment required in every prison in the land? The answer is lack of funding.

## Researching a Chemical Cure for Craving and Addiction

The third leg of the stool of a bilateral harm reduction drug policy, along with education and treatment, would be a dramatic increase in both the funding and focus of research to attack the problem of addiction. Embryonic programs under way at present could be accelerated and enhanced with the additional funding provided by the legalized sale of drugs. A truly big-league national research budget would hasten the day when medications for the prevention and treatment of addiction are available.

George F. Will, the Washington columnist, observed years ago:

*By now, given how much we know about brain chemistry, we probably should have a technological response to the destructive*

*forces unleashed by 19th-century chemistry. Government sup-
port should have provided the resources (and prestige; that
matters in science) for research to discover chemical compounds
that block or reverse the pleasure-and-addiction-producing
effects of drugs. Is it too much to ask that this be taken as
seriously by medical researchers as AIDS is?*[23]

From the other end of the political spectrum, Daniel Patrick
Moynihan, the Democratic senator from New York, wrote that the
drug problem presented society with two unpalatable alternatives:
"an enormous public health problem [or] an enormous crime problem." Liking neither choice, he urged medical research to vigorously
pursue a chemical "blocking or neutralizing agent" to help drug
abusers move "as near to abstinence as possible."[24]

## Cocaine Research

Because cocaine and its derivative, crack, have received so much
attention in the media, finding a pharmaceutical aid to the cocaine
problem should be the highest priority among drug researchers.
Kenneth Blum, a professor of pharmacology at the University of
Texas, and Ernest Noble, a professor of alcohol studies at UCLA,
found gene patterns suggesting a predisposition to addiction in both
severe alcoholics and cocaine addicts.[25] The gene patterns are related
to dopamine, an agent in the brain that plays a role in creating
pleasure sensations. In spite of limited funding, this most promising
research centering around dopamine and its role as the chemical
conductor in the brain goes on.

In another area of research, scientists have developed an artifi-
cial enzyme capable of reducing the addictive effects of cocaine: The
new enzyme destroys most of the cocaine in the bloodstream before
it reaches the brain. This greatly reduces the degree of intoxication as
well as the dependence potential of the drug. Dr. Donald W. Landry,

who has been working on his theory for more than six years, feels that it has real potential to produce a "shot-in-the-arm" treatment for cocaine addiction.[26]

## Heroin Research: A Tough Nut

The most dangerous of the popular illegal drugs because it is the only truly addictive drug of the big three, heroin is also the least used. As with all drugs, use does not necessarily mean abuse, but because of the strong addictive qualities of the drug and its attraction to the most reckless of drug users, it has the largest ratio of addicts to users.

In 1992, researchers from UCLA and the Hebrew University of Jerusalem, in separate studies, isolated two key elements of the body's pain-control system. The hope is that now, researchers will be able to separate the painkilling qualities of the opiates from their addictive qualities, leading to a nonaddictive version of heroin. "The long search for new painkillers that will not produce drug dependence and withdrawal can now be logically pursued," said Dr. Floyd E. Bloom, a neuropharmacologist at the Scripps Research Institute in La Jolla, California.[27]

Research needs some tub thumping to energize public interest groups and the addiction treatment field itself to advocate for more research, much as has happened with the AIDS cause. According to Robert Curley, national editor of *Alcoholism & Drug Abuse Weekly*, "Addiction prevention is represented [in Washington] by exactly one part-time lobbyist . . . and I don't know of anyone who advocates directly on behalf of addiction research."[28] The National Academy of Sciences is calling for a fundamental change to elevate the development priority of new medications: "We are recommending the creation of a system of centers involved in drug research, similar to the cancer centers of the National Institutes of Health."[29] The funding available from a harm control approach to drugs would make this possible.

## Would the Drug Problem Worsen Under Legalization? What About the Children?

Many Americans believe that legalization or any softening of the hard line on drug prohibition would inevitably lead to greatly increased drug use, yet there is no evidence of this. On the contrary, existing data indicate that legalization would have a minimal effect on the number of drug users and abusers. For example, two polls, one a collaborative effort by the University of Connecticut and the *Hartford Courant* newspaper and the other done for the Drug Policy Foundation of Washington, D.C., showed that less than 4 percent of respondents would be interested in trying any now-illegal drug should it be legalized.[30]

Writing in *The New England Journal of Medicine,* Drs. Lester Grinspoon and James B. Bakalar of the Harvard Medical School offered this analysis: "Only 2 percent of people who do not use cocaine say they might try it if it were legalized, and 93 percent state vehemently that they would not."[31]

As for children, an integral part of a harm reduction strategy would be the strictly enforced prohibition of drug sales to persons under 21. Heavy sanctions would be imposed on anyone making drugs available to underage children. While it would be naive to suppose that minors will not illegally obtain some drugs, just as they do today with alcohol and cigarettes, we should not delude ourselves about their availability under prohibition. Ernie, a teenage marijuana smoker, said:

> *I figured it was a lot easier to smoke dope than it was to drink, because dope is easier to hide and it's a lot easier to get. There's no such thing as being "under age." You don't have to have an ID to buy pot or hash, and it's available everywhere — at school, at the shopping center, in the gym, at concerts, in the park. Everywhere. To score, all you have to do is hang out.*[32]

Statistics from the University of Michigan's 1997 annual study of the nation's high school population indicate that Ernie's experience is not unique. Its figures show how many high school seniors surveyed thought the following drugs were "fairly easy" or "very easy" to get: marijuana, 90 percent; cocaine, 49 percent; LSD, 51 percent; and heroin, 34 percent.[33]

Government has a contract with the governed that it will protect the young to the best of its ability. While its ability to do so is limited, and parents obviously have the fundamental responsibility for such protection, it would be a serious breach of governmental responsibility to allow the sale of drugs to minors. Some will assert that a black market will supply that demand. That is no more likely to happen with drugs than it has with alcohol and tobacco.

## Leadership Is the Key

Any discussion of changing government's role vis-à-vis drugs must address changing our laws. Repeal of alcohol prohibition after 14 years is a monument to the American people's ability to admit and correct a mistake. Today's war on drugs has been waged for a quarter of a century with little or no success. The inescapable question is: How much longer will we persist with this failed policy? Every administration in the last 50 years has felt itself locked up in an Alcatraz of public opinion and thus compelled to approach the drug problem with a "nail 'em and jail 'em" policy, resulting in the imprisonment of over a million of our citizens each year for drug-related offenses.

As long as humans continue as imperfect creatures, humans will use drugs. Our leaders are left with the task of minimizing the harm done by drugs in the context of that unpleasant reality. One of the enormous burdens of leadership is the imperative of selecting a course of action from a set of imperfect alternatives. Thus did President Truman decide to drop the first atomic bombs to end World War II, and Abraham Lincoln make decisions that led to the Civil War.

Alonzo L. McDonald, in his foreword to *Abraham Lincoln: Theologian of American Anguish*, wrote, more than 100 years after Lincoln's death:

> *Lincoln was a master in understanding the paradox of choosing between "the lesser of two evils." He recognized well that frequently there is no feasible, absolutely "right" answer. Therefore he considered it the responsibility of the leader to move firmly and consistently along paths that may not have been ideal in themselves . . . but which represented pragmatic steps advancing the lesser of two evils.*[34]

The drug issue requires from our leaders the courage and wisdom to recognize the problem's inevitability. Does that mean that its present form and pervasiveness are inevitable? Certainly not, but any hope of progress presupposes that we work intelligently and with attainable objectives in mind.

Opinions on our response to the drug problem are divided by ferocious polarities. At one pole we have the defenders of the status quo who believe that the war on drugs is both necessary and worthwhile in spite of its obvious failure. At the other are those who recognize that in order to make any progress, we must change — like it or not. Strong leadership can break this impasse, and that leadership must come from the President and the Congress of the United States.

The noted British historian, Paul Johnson, salutes the leadership imperative of choosing between imperfect alternatives with these words:

> *[Some] politicians have tended to display bad political judgment in twentieth-century democracies because they refuse to accept the hard reality that the search for the perfect is the enemy of the good. This is not an argument for moral nihilism*

*or relativism. But the application of moral principles to com-
plex and ambiguous circumstances requires the cautious judgment of statesmen who recognize that the art of politics is the
ability to find not the perfect solution but the best solution in
an imperfect world.*[35]

# NOTES

## Chapter 1: Drug Users and Drugs: Myths Versus Facts

1. Dan Waldorf, Craig Reinarman, Sheigla Murphy, *Cocaine Changes* (Philadelphia: Temple University Press, 1991), p. 2.
2. Robert Reno, "What's Wrong with Discussing Drugs?" *Miami Herald,* Dec. 16, 1993.
3. Bob Curley, "Addiction Insights," *Alcoholism and Drug Abuse Weekly,* April 3, 1995, p. 5.
4. Marianne W. Zawitz, ed., *Drugs, Crime, and the Justice System* (Washington, D.C.: U.S. Department of Justice, 1992), p. 25.
5. Sally Jacobs, "Lowell Police Dragnet Highlights Suburban Drug Use," *Boston Globe,* July 18, 1993.
6. Benjamin Weiser, "Wall St.: High Pressure, High Powered, Often Just High," *Washington Post,* May 13, 1994.
7. *Los Angeles Times,* Oct. 31, 1993.
8. Melanie E. Bennett and Barbara S. McCready, "Comorbid Subtyping Points to Youths' Different Treatment Needs," *Brown University Digest of Addiction Theory and Application,* August 1994, p. 4.
9. Michael W. Miller, "Mental Patients Fight to Smoke in the Hospital," *Wall Street Journal,* Oct. 11, 1994.
10. Waldorf, Reinarman, Murphy, p. 2.
11. Ibid., p. 10.
12. Ibid., p. 192.
13. "ONDCP Profiles 2.1 Million Hard-Core Cocaine Users," *Alcoholism and Drug Abuse Weekly,* Aug. 16, 1993, p. 4.
14. Ronald J. Ostrow, "War on Drugs Shifting Its Focus to Hard-Core Addicts," *Chicago Sun-Times,* Oct. 20, 1993.
15. Ibid.

16. Douglas N. Husak, "Can Drug Laws Be Justified as Anticipatory Offenses?" in *Strategies for Change*, ed. Arnold S. Trebach and Kevin B. Zeese (Washington, D.C.: Drug Policy Foundation Press, 1992), p. 93.

17. Mark Thornton, *The Economics of Prohibition: Everything You Need to Know About Mind-Altering Drugs* (Salt Lake City: University of Utah Press, 1991), p. 91.

18. Waldorf, Reinarman, Murphy, p. 302.

19. Peter Reuter, "Hawks Ascendant: The Punitive Trend of American Drug Policy," in *Daedalus, Political Pharmacology: Thinking About Drugs*, ed. Stephen R. Graubard, Vol. 121, No. 3 (1992), p. 33.

20. Benjamin H. Renshaw III and Sue A. Lindgren, *Drugs and Crime Facts 1994* (Washington, D.C.: Bureau of Justice Statistics, 1995), p. 30.

21. Waldorf, Reinarman, Murphy, p. 35.

22. Andrew Weil and Winifred Rosen, *From Chocolate to Morphine: Everything You Need to Know About Mind-Altering Drugs* (Boston: Houghton Mifflin, 1993), p. 50.

23. Waldorf, Reinarman, Murphy, p. 274.

24. Stanton Peele, *The Meaning of Addiction* (Lexington, Mass.: Lexington Books, 1985), p. 6.

25. Table based on Robert Byck, "Cocaine, Marijuana, and the Meanings of Addiction," in *Dealing with Drugs*, ed. Ronald Hamowy (San Francisco: Pacific Research Institute for Public Policy, 1987), p. 244, Table 6-1.

26. *National Household Survey on Drug Abuse 1996*, Washington, D.C.: U.S. Department of Health and Human Services, www.health.org, January 20, 1998.

27. S. Robert Lichter and Linda Lichter, eds., *Media Monitor*, July–August 1997, p. 4.

28. Rudy Abramson, "Tobacco Country," *Los Angeles Times*, Dec. 4, 1994.

29. Office of National Drug Control Policy, "Consumption Approach to Cocaine and Heroin," www.whitehousedrugpolicy.gov, Jan. 20, 1998, p. 3.

30. Carolyn Skorneck, "Treatment Best Weapon in Cocaine War: Study," *Chicago Sun-Times*, June 14, 1994.

31. Steven Wisotsky, "Images of Death and Destruction in Drug Law Cases," in The Great Issues of Drug Policy, ed. Arnold S. Trebach and Devin B. Zeese (Washington, D.C.: Drug Policy Foundation, 1990), p. 54.

32. Yih-Img Hser, M. Douglas Anglin, Keiko Powers, "Natural History of Narcotics Addiction Somewhat Stable," *Brown University Digest of Addiction Theory and Application*, January 1994, p. 5.

33. Zawitz, p. 37.

34. Ibid., p. 40.

35. Ibid., p. 145.
36. James Bovard, *Lost Rights* (New York: St. Martin's Press, 1994), p. 204.
37. Terry Williams, *Crackhouse* (Reading, Mass.: Addison-Wesley, 1992), p. 8.
38. Office of National Drug Control Policy, "Consumption Approach," Table 4.
39. Candice Byrne, *Drugs and Crime Data* (Washington, D.C.: Office of National Drug Control Policy, 1996), p. 4.
40. Jose de Cordoba, "Death in Colombia," *Wall Street Journal*, Dec. 3, 1993.
41. Zawitz, p. 26.
42. Trish Power, "Heroin Makes a Comeback; Number of Overdoses Rising," *Miami Herald*, June 28, 1993.
43. Ibid.
44. Sam Vincent Meddis, "Smack's Back," *USA Today*, May 25, 1994.
45. Sandy Rovner, "Drug Habits of Young Adults," *Washington Post*, July 27, 1993.
46. Weil and Rosen, p. 114.
47. Michael Pollan, "Marijuana in the 90s," *The New York Times Magazine*, Feb. 19, 1995, p. 34.
48. Ibid., p. 56.
49. Weil and Rosen, p. 119.
50. Eliot Marshall, *Legalization: A Debate* (New York: Chelsea House, 1988), p. 57.
51. Ibid., p. 56.
52. Cate Chant, "Students at UMass Vote 2–1 for Pot," *Boston Globe*, March 12, 1993.
53. Weil and Rosen, p. 120.
54. Zawitz, p. 27.
55. Ibid.
56. Peele, p. 8.
57. Ibid., p. 144.
58. Ibid., p. 144.
59. Weil and Rosen, p. 11.

## Chapter 2: Other Illegal Drugs

1. "Country Singer Tells Congress Treatment Is Key to Stemming Drug Use," *Narcotics Control Digest*, June 8, 1994, p. 10.
2. Alexander T. Shulgin, *Controlled Substances* (Berkeley, Calif.: Ronin Publishing, 1992), p. 5.
3. Jenifer Warren, "LSD Makes a Return Trip," *Los Angeles Times*, April 16, 1993, p. A3.

4. Ibid.
5. "Judicial Panel Proposes Cap on Drug Sentences," *USA Today,* March 22, 1993.
6. James Bovard, *Lost Rights* (New York: St. Martin's Press, 1994), p. 210.
7. Joyce Buchanan, University of Michigan press release, Dec. 18, 1997, Table 1a.
8. Ibid, Table 7.
9. Jack Anderson and Michael Binstein, "Home-Grown Drug Menace," *Washington Post,* Oct. 10, 1993.
10. Judy Pasternak, "Despite Crackdown, 'Cat' Is Spreading Across Midwest," *Los Angeles Times,* Oct. 23, 1994.
11. "Cat Problem Spreads Throughout the U.S.," *Narcotics Control Digest,* Sept. 14, 1994, p. 4.
12. Ibid.
13. Anderson and Binstein, "Home-Grown Drug Menace."
14. "Cat Poses National Threat, Experts Say," *Alcoholism and Drug Abuse Weekly,* Dec. 13, 1993, p. 5.
15. Lester Grinspoon and James B. Bakalar, "Medical Uses of Illicit Drugs," in *Dealing with Drugs,* ed. Ronald Hamowy (San Francisco: Pacific Research Institute for Public Policy, 1987), p. 194.
16. Mark Arax and Tom Gorman, "California's Illicit Farm Belt Export," *Los Angeles Times,* March 3, 1995.
17. Mark Arax and Tom Gorman, "Powerful People Have Been Users of Dangerous Drugs," *Los Angeles Times,* March 13, 1995.
18. Ibid.
19. Thomas A. Constantine, "Mexican Traffickers Muscle In on Methamphetamine Manufacturing, Smuggling," *Narcotics Control Digest,* Aug. 31, 1994, p. 2.
20. Stanton Peele, *The Meaning of Addiction* (Lexington, Mass.: Lexington Books, 1985), p. 139.
21. Weil and Rosen, *From Chocolate to Morphine,* p. 137.
22. Randy E. Barnett, "Curing the Drug-Law Addiction," in Hamowy, *Dealing with Drugs,* p. 84.

## Chapter 3: Money Is Indeed the Root of This Evil

1. Gustavo de Greiff, "Enforce the Drug Laws, but Start Contemplating Legalization Now," *Drug Policy Letter of the Drug Policy Foundation,* Spring 1994, p. 6.
2. Ibid., p. 28.
3. "Illicit Drug Spending Fell in '95, Office Says," *Los Angeles Times,* Nov. 10, 1997.

4. Dennis Cauchon, "Biden: Shift Drug Focus to User," *USA Today,* April 30, 1993.

5. Nora Zamichow, "Marijuana Growers Take Root in Southland's Remote Areas," *Los Angeles Times,* Sept. 25, 1992.

6. "Nationwide Heroin, Marijuana Use Rising," *Narcotics Control Digest,* May 25, 1994, p. 1.

7. "South American Drug Production Increases," *Forensic Drug Abuse Advisor,* March 1997, p. 18.

8. Ibid.

9. "Amount, Purity of Heroin Increasing in Massachusetts," *Narcotics Control Digest,* May 26, 1993, p. 1.

10. Mark Thornton, *The Economics of Prohibition* (Salt Lake City: University of Utah Press, 1991), p. 90.

11. Ibid., p. 91.

12. Steven Wisotsky, *Beyond the War on Drugs* (Buffalo: Prometheus Books, 1990), p. 36.

13. Ibid.

14. Carol J. Boyd, "Sexual Abuse Precedes Women's Depression, Crack Abuse," *Brown University Digest of Addiction Theory and Application,* March 1994, p. 1.

15. David Cox, "Bill for Drug Generation's Indulgence Is Coming Due," *Miami Herald,* June 17, 1994.

16. Richard J. Dennis, "The American People Are Starting to Question the Drug War," in *Drug Prohibition and the Conscience of Nations,* ed. Arnold S. Trebach and Kevin B. Zeese (Washington, D.C.: Drug Policy Foundation, 1990), p. 221.

17. Marcia Slacum Greene, "Pushing Hope on the Street," *Washington Post,* Oct. 9, 1993.

18. Paul Valentine, "Pushing Back in Baltimore," *Washington Post,* Nov. 27, 1993.

19. John Paul Newport, Jr., "Steps to Help the Urban Black Man," *Fortune,* Dec. 18, 1989, p. 119.

20. Ibid.

21. Tim Wells and William Triplett, *Drug Wars: An Oral History from the Trenches* (New York: William Morrow, 1992), p. 45.

22. Ibid., p. 85.

23. Tom Dubocq, "Race Tycoon Arrested on Drug Charges," *Miami Herald,* Nov. 23, 1993.

24. Marianne W. Zawitz, ed., *Drugs, Crime, and the Justice System* (Washington, D.C.: U.S. Department of Justice, 1992), p. 62.

25. William C. Rempel, "Taking the Cartels to the Cleaners," *Los Angeles Times,* July 4, 1993.
26. G. Bruce Knecht, "Case Is Settled by American Express Unit," *Wall Street Journal,* Nov. 22, 1994.
27. "Professionals Busted in International Laundering Ring," *Narcotics Control Digest,* Dec. 7, 1994, p. 6.
28. Ibid.
29. John J. Fialka, "Drug Smugglers Export Dollars to Evade Law," *Wall Street Journal,* April 7, 1994.
30. Sam Enriquez, "Former Courier Describes Smuggling of $50 Million Inside Appliances," *Los Angeles Times,* Dec. 11, 1992.
31. Rempel, "Taking the Cartels," p. A16.
32. Lally Weymouth, "Organized Crime: The New Russian Menace," *Washington Post,* Dec. 28, 1993.
33. Andrew Higgins, "Drug Money Finances Nuclear Program," *San Francisco Examiner,* June 17, 1994.

## Chapter 4: Societal Harm from Drug Money

1. Mark Thornton, *The Economics of Prohibition* (Salt Lake City: University of Utah Press, 1991), p. 128.
2. Tim Wells and William Triplett, *Drug Wars: An Oral History from the Trenches* (New York: William Morrow, 1992), p. 101.
3. Sebastian Rotella, "Two Inspectors at Border Charged in Drug Probe," *Los Angeles Times,* February 14, 1995.
4. "New Orleans Officers Indicted on Drug, Gun Charges," *Los Angeles Times,* Dec. 8, 1994.
5. Ruben Castaneda, "D.C. Jail Workers Charged with Taking Bribes, Transporting Drugs," *Washington Post,* Nov. 5, 1993.
6. "Last of Fugitive Miami Police Surrenders to FBI," *Narcotics Control Digest,* Feb. 2, 1994, p. 9.
7. A series of in-depth articles by Victor Merina for the *Los Angeles Times* (December 1, 2, 3, 1993) provided much of the background information on the Los Angeles County Sheriff's Department scandal. Other *L.A. Times* articles by Merina that the author consulted are the following: "Deputy Pleads Guilty to Money Laundering," May 18, 1993; "The Slide from Cop to Criminal," Dec. 1, 1993; "Anonymous Note Alerted Sheriff to Deputies' Thefts," Dec. 2, 1993; "Deputies' Downfall Began with a Videotaped Sting," Dec. 3, 1993.

Articles by Kenneth Reich, also of the *L.A. Times*, were also consulted: "Two More Ex-Deputies Sentenced in Drug Money Case," Oct. 11, 1993; "Three More Former Deputies Guilty in Skimming," Aug. 30, 1994; "Two Ex-Deputies Convicted in Drug Money Case," Feb. 22, 1995.

8. Malcolm Gladwell, "In Drug War, Crime Sometimes Wears a Badge," *Washington Post*, May 19, 1994.

9. Mark Fineman, "Mexico Releases Three Suspects Arrested in Latest Slaying," *Los Angeles Times*, May 12, 1995.

10. Tod Robberson, "Mexican Held in U.S. Linked to Drug Cartel," *Washington Post*, March 9, 1995.

11. Mark Fineman, "Mexico Widens Dragnet for Drug Lords," *Los Angeles Times*, May 14, 1995.

12. Ibid.

13. Russell Watson et al., "Death on the Spot," *Newsweek*, Dec. 13, 1993, p. 19.

14. Thornton, p. 136.

15. Marianne W. Zawitz, ed., *Drugs, Crime, and the Justice System* (Washington, D.C.: U.S. Department of Justice, 1992), p. 6.

16. Dan Waldorf, Craig Reinarman, Sheigla Murphy, *Cocaine Changes* (Philadelphia: Temple University Press, 1991), p. 302.

17. Joseph B. Treaster, "48 Indicted in Gang Warfare over Drugs," *New York Times*, June 23, 1994.

18. "64 Alleged Members of $50M Drug Gang Indicted in NYC," *Narcotics Control Digest*, Oct. 12, 1994, p. 3.

19. Ibid., p. 4.

20. Arnold Markowitz, "Police Smash Crack Ring at Scott Housing Project," *Miami Herald*, June 8, 1993.

21. Ron Harris, "The Price We Pay for Donovan's Addiction," *Los Angeles Times*, Aug. 20, 1993.

## Chapter 5: Civil Liberties: The War Within the War on Drugs

1. William F. Buckley, Jr., *Happy Times Were Here Again* (New York: Random House, 1993), p. 185.

2. James Bovard, *Lost Rights* (New York: St. Martin's Press, 1994), p. 215.

3. Milton Friedman and Thomas S. Szasz, *On Liberty and Drugs* (Washington, D.C.: Drug Policy Foundation Press, 1992), p. 3.

4. Steven Wisotsky, "Views from the Criminal Justice System," in *The Great Issues of Drug Policy*, ed. Arnold S. Trebach and Kevin B. Zeese (Washington, D.C.: Drug Policy Foundation, 1990), p. 56.

5. Thom Mrozek, "Unusual Police Powers Lead to Conviction," *Los Angeles Times*, Aug. 25, 1993.

6. Timothy Williams, "Street Barriers Backfired, Critics Say," *Los Angeles Times*, June 28, 1993.

7. Jim Herron Zamora, "Police Use Warning Letters in War on Drugs," *Los Angeles Times*, Aug. 3, 1992.

8. "Ohio Drug Confiscations Total $47 Million," *Narcotics Control Digest*, Dec. 22, 1993, p. 10.

9. Bovard, p. 209.

10. Ibid., p. 206.

11. Debbie Howlett, "Chicago Ready To Hang Up on Corner Drug Dealers," *USA Today*, October 5, 1994.

12. Bovard, p. 209.

13. Marlene Cimons, "U.S. Officials Urge Opiate Use to Ease Cancer Pain If Needed," *Los Angeles Times*, March 3, 1994.

14. "Fears of Addiction Contribute to Needless Suffering of Pain," *Alcoholism and Drug Abuse Weekly*, Nov. 14, 1994, p. 7.

15. Marlene Cimons, "U.S. to Review Medicinal Marijuana Ban," *Los Angeles Times*, Jan. 6, 1994.

16. Pamela Ferdinand, "Medical Marijuana: A Renewed Push," *Miami Herald*, April 8, 1993.

17. "Medicinal Marijuana Ban Gets White House Review," *San Francisco Examiner*, Jan. 5, 1994.

18. Richard C. Paddock, "Is Smoking Pot Good Medicine?" *Los Angeles Times*, Feb. 26, 1995.

19. Joseph Berger, "Mother's Drug Arrest Sends Her on Crusade," *New York Times*, Oct. 11, 1993.

20. Kenny Jenks, "Before I Go," in *Strategies for Change*, ed. Arnold S. Trebach and Kevin B. Zeese (Washington, D.C.: Drug Policy Foundation Press, 1992), p. 215.

21. "White House Drug Policy Chief to Meet with Colombia's Samper," *Narcotics Enforcement and Prevention Digest*, Oct. 9, 1997, p. 3.

22. Carl Ingram, " 'Smoke a Joint, Lose License' Law in Effect," *Los Angeles Times*, Dec. 1, 1994.

23. Ibid.

24. "N.Y. Appeals Court Says State Must Prove Defendants Knew Weight of Drugs," *Narcotics Control Digest*, Jan. 5, 1994, p. 8.

25. Todd Hartman, "Court Ruling May Doom Taxes on Drug Profits," *Miami Herald*, April 22, 1993.

26. Paul M. Barrett, "Supreme Court Limits Application of Drug 'Taxes,'" *Wall Street Journal*, June 7, 1994.
27. Linda Greenhouse, "Justices Consider Drug Tax Tactics," *New York Times*, Jan. 20, 1994.
28. Marianne W. Zawitz, ed., *Drugs, Crime, and the Justice System* (Washington, D.C.: U.S. Department of Justice, 1992), p. 54.
29. Greenhouse.
30. "N.C. Leads Nation in Taxing Illegal Drug Traffic," *Narcotics Enforcement and Prevention Digest*, May 29, 1997, p. 7.
31. Bovard, p. 11.
32. Andrew Schneider and Mary Pat Flaherty, "Police Profit by Seizing Homes of Innocent," in *Presumed Guilty* (Pittsburgh: Scripps Howard News Service, 1991), p. 16.
33. Thomas Grillo, "Drug War Spoils Create Divide," *Boston Globe*, Dec. 11, 1993.
34. Ibid.
35. Robert E. Bauman, "Take It Away," *National Review*, Feb. 20, 1995, p. 36. Matt Carroll, "Government Home Seizures," *Boston Globe*, July 4, 1993.
36. "Asset Forfeiture" DEA Publications Briefing Book, www.usdoj.gov/dea/pubs/briefing 3-13 htm. January 27, 1998.
37. Bauman, p. 35.
38. Ibid., p. 36.
39. Bovard, p. 16.
40. Ibid., p. 17.
41. "Innocent Citizens May Keep Drug-Financed Items," *Miami Herald*, Feb. 25, 1993.
42. Matthew Brelis, "Boston Defense Lawyers Laud Seizure Ruling," *Boston Globe*, June 29, 1993.
43. Bovard, p. 17.
44. David G. Savage, "Court Curbs Power to Seize Property of Drug Dealers," *Los Angeles Times*, June 29, 1993.
45. Bauman, p. 38.

## Chapter 6: Can We Be Both Free and Drug-Free?

1. "Drug Dealers Beware: The Lawyers Are Coming," *Alcoholism and Drug Abuse Weekly*, March 14, 1994, p. 5.
2. Arnold Ceballos, "New State Laws Let People Sue Drug Dealer," *Wall Street Journal*, July 16, 1996.
3. "In the Courts," *Narcotics Control Digest*, Aug. 3, 1994, p. 6.

4. James C. McKinley, Jr., "Court Calls a Sentence Too Harsh," *New York Times,* Feb. 3, 1995.
5. Lee Romney and Kevin Johnson, "Police Crime Lab Making Cocaine for Drug Busts," *Los Angeles Times,* Oct. 21, 1994.
6. "Man Sues over Drug Sting," *Narcotics Control Digest,* Jan. 5, 1994, p. 7.
7. Romney and Johnson, "Police Crime Lab," p. A27.
8. Julie Stewart, "Mandatory Minimum Cases," fact sheet distributed by Families Against Minimum Sentences Foundation, Washington, D.C., 1993.
9. "Three Officers in Botched Boston Raid Also Accused in Another Civil Rights Case," *Narcotics Control Digest,* April 27, 1994, p. 5.
10. Joe Hallinan, "Ill-Aimed Drug Raids Leave Trail of Victims," *San Francisco Examiner-Chronicle,* Oct. 10, 1993.
11. Ibid.
12. Beth Shuster, "L.A. Schools Weigh Rewards for Student Informants," *Los Angeles Times,* Feb. 9, 1995.
13. "Appeals Court OKs Expanded Drug Testing for Customs Workers," *Narcotics Control Digest,* July 20, 1994, p. 8.
14. Ronald Hamowy, "Illicit Drugs and Government Control" *Dealing with Drugs,* ed. R. Hamowy (San Francisco: Pacific Research Institute for Public Policy, 1987), p. 5.
15. "1996 AMA Survey — Workplace Drug Testing and Drug Abuse Policies — Summary of Key Findings," American Management Association, New York, p. 1.
16. Richard Saltus, "Workplace Drug Tests Questioned," *Boston Globe,* Nov. 30, 1993.
17. Hamowy, p. 7.
18. Francis X. Clines, "Drug Law Catching Few Kingpins," *New York Times,* March 23, 1993.
19. Hamowy, p. 7.
20. Michael Pollan, "Marijuana in the 90's," *The New York Times Magazine,* Feb. 19, 1995, p. 32.
21. U.S. vs. Patillo, *93 Daily Journal* D.A.R. 5399, March 23, 1993.
22. "Arrests for Drug Abuse Violations by Age Group, 1970–96", Bureau of Justice statistics, U.S. Department of Justice, F.B.I. Uniform Crime Report, http://www.ojp.usdoj.gov/bjs/glance/drugar.
23. Saundra Torry, "Some Federal Judges Just Say No to Drug Cases," *Washington Post,* May 17, 1993.
24. Duke Helfand, "They're Cleaning Up in Court," *Los Angeles Times* (Long Beach Supplement), March 3, 1994.

25. Martin Finucane, "Advocates for Poor Hit Drug-Related Eviction," *Chicago Sun-Times*, Dec. 22, 1993.
26. Art Golab, "CHA Aims to Evict Parents of Truants," *Chicago Sun-Times*, Nov. 17, 1993.
27. Ronald Brownstein, "Frisk for Guns at Housing Projects, Panel Urges," *Los Angeles Times*, April 13, 1994.
28. Kevin G. Salwen, "White House Proposal Allows Searches Without Warrants in Public Housing," *Wall Street Journal*, April 18, 1994.
29. Judy Foreman, "Pregnant Drug Use Shown to Be 1 in 10," *Boston Globe*, Sept. 16, 1993.
30. Paul Taubman, "Externalities and Decriminalization of Drugs," in *Searching for Alternatives*, ed. Melvyn B. Krauss and Edward P. Lazear (Stanford, Calif.: Hoover Institution Press, 1991), p. 98.
31. Charles Lusane, *Pipe Dream Blues: Racism and the War on Drugs* (Boston: South End Press, 1991), p. 59.
32. Ibid.
33. Barry Siegel, "In the Name of the Children," *Los Angeles Times Magazine*, Aug. 7, 1994, p. 14.
34. Ibid.
35. Maribeth Vander Weele, "Cocaine Kids Come of Age," *Chicago Sun-Times*, July 6, 1994.
36. Ibid.
37. D. Barone, "Wednesday's Child: Literary Development of Children Prenatally Exposed to Crack Cocaine," *The Brown University Digest of Addiction Theory* and *Application*, March 1994, p. 8.

## Chapter 7: The Inundation of Our Police, Courts, and Prisons

1. Tim Wells and William Triplett, *Drug Wars: An Oral History from the Trenches* (New York: William Morrow, 1992), p. 11.
2. Marianne W. Zawitz, ed., *Drugs, Crime, and the Justice System* (Washington, D.C.: U.S. Department of Justice, 1992), p. 6.
3. Charles G. Cole et al., *The State of Criminal Justice* (Washington, D.C.: American Bar Association, 1993), p. 4.
4. Ronald Hamowy, ed., *Dealing with Drugs* (San Francisco: Pacific Research Institute for Public Policy, 1987), p. 14.
5. Eliot Marshall, *Legalization: A Debate* (New York: Chelsea House, 1988), p. 28.

6. "Police Must Wait 15 Seconds Before Breaking Down Doors," *Narcotics Control Digest*, Sept. 29, 1993, p. 4.

7. "Heroin Smuggling Sentences Imposed," *San Francisco Examiner*, Oct. 14, 1993.

8. "Military's Image Better Than Religion's, Poll Finds," *Los Angeles Times*, May 29, 1993.

9. Wells and Triplett, p. 203.

10. Ibid., p. 207.

11. Charles L. Lindner, "A Tale of Two Trials — and the Fate of a City," *Los Angeles Times*, April 4, 1993.

12. H. G. Reza, "Drug Runners Arrested at Border Often Go Free," *Los Angeles Times*, May 12, 1996.

13. Peter Reuter, "The Punitive Trend of American Drug Policy," *Daedalus, Political Pharmacology: Thinking About Drugs*, ed. Stephen R. Graubard, (Summer 1992, Vol. 121, No. 3), p. 27.

14. Joseph R. Biden, Jr., the staff of the International American Drug Strategy, and the staff of the Senate Judiciary Committee, *America's Drug Strategy* (Washington, D.C.) p. 41.

15. Dennis Cauchon, "Dual Prosecution Can Give One Crime Two Punishments," *USA Today*, March 29, 1993.

16. Ibid.

17. Wells and Triplett, p. 11.

18. "Northeast Drug Sweep Turns Into Street Fight," *Washington Times*, July 22, 1993.

19. Stephen A. Fisher, "Illegal Drugs and the Outlaw Hero Mythology," in *Strategies for Change*, ed. Arnold S. Trebach and Kevin B. Zeese (Washington, D.C.: Drug Policy Foundation Press, 1992), p. 121.

20. Jerome H. Skolnick, "Rethinking the Drug Problem," in *Daedalus — Political Pharmacology*, p. 150.

21. Miles Corwin, "Police Officers Find Their Task Increasingly Perilous," *Los Angeles Times*, March 20, 1993, p. A-1.

22. Randy E. Barnett, "Curing the Drug Law Addiction," in Hamowy, *Dealing with Drugs*, p. 89.

23. Andy Furillo, "Bolinas on Edge After Drug Agents Bust LSD Ring," *San Francisco Examiner-Chronicle*, Sept. 12, 1993.

24. David M. Kennedy, *Closing the Market* (Washington, D.C.: National Institute of Justice, 1993), p. 8.

25. Errol Smith, "Call Out the Guard to Put the Lid on L.A. Crime," *Los Angeles Times*, Sept. 5, 1993.

26. Henry R. Wray et al, *Confronting the Drug Problem* (Washington, D.C.: United States General Accounting Office, 1993), p. 19.

27. Jeff Kramer, "Drug War: New Front Out West", *Boston Globe*, August 9, 1993.

28. Steven B. Duke, "How Legalization Would Cut Crime," *Los Angeles Times*, December 21, 1993.

29. "More Drug Offenses Key in Record Prison Rolls," *Narcotics Enforcement and Prevention Digest*, June 26, 1997, p. 1.

30. "U.S. Prison Population Slowed in '96," *Los Angeles Times*, June 23, 1997.

31. Cole et al., p. 6.

32. Robert L. Jackson, "Dangers to Prison Guards Rise as Inmates' Conditions Worsen," *Los Angeles Times*, May 7, 1993.

33. Julie Stewart, "Crime Bill is Just 'Feel Good' Legislation," *USA Today*, November 15, 1993.

34. "Prisoners in 1996 — Highlights," U.S. Department of Justice, Bureau of Justice Statistics, Washington, D.C., June 1997, NCJ 164619, p. 1, (son.soci.miu.edu/crit crim/prisons/pris 96.txt).

35. Zawitz, *Drugs, Crime and Justice*, p. 201.

36. Clarence Lusane, *Pipe Dream Blues: Racism and the War on Drugs* (Boston: South End Press, 1991), p. 69.

37. "Attorney General Pledges More Cooperation with Local Agencies," *Narcotics Control Digest*, Dec. 22, 1993, p. 3.

38. Jeffrey A. Hoffman, "Alternative Drug Treatment," *Washington Post*, Sept. 26, 1993.

39. Wray, p. 35.

40. Deborah Sharp, "Innovative Ideas Win Praise in Florida," *USA Today*, March 9, 1993.

41. Biden, p. 47.

42. Wray, p. 29.

43. Laura E. Drager et al., "Drug Treatment Referral in Criminal Courts Must Continue," *New York Times*, Aug. 5, 1993.

44. Editorial, "A New Approach to Drug Crime," *Los Angeles Times*, May 5, 1997.

## Chapter 8: Race Relations and Drugs: A Grim Prospect

1. Everett Carll Ladd, "Racial Equality in America," *Christian Science Monitor*, Jan. 12, 1990; telephone conversation with Tom W. Smith of NORC, University of Chicago, Dec. 1, 1997.

2. Kathleen Maguire and Ann L. Pastore, eds., *Bureau of Justice Statistics*

*Sourcebook of Criminal Justice Statistics — 1993* (Albany: Hindelang Criminal Justice Research Center, State University of New York, 1994), pp. 344, 432.

3. Douglas S. Massey and Nancy A. Denton, *American Apartheid* (Cambridge, Mass.: Harvard University Press, 1993).

4. Derrick Z. Jackson, "Segregated Tales from the Drug Underworld," *Boston Globe,* July 28, 1993.

5. Joe Davidson, "Bill to Equalize Cocaine Penalties Faces Tough Fight," *Wall Street Journal,* April 13, 1995.

6. David G. Savage, "Clinton OKs Bill Keeping Stiff Sentences for Crack," *Los Angeles Times,* Oct. 31, 1995.

7. Robert L. Jackson, "Panel Urges More Parity in Cocaine Sentences," *Los Angeles Times,* April 30, 1997.

8. Carrell Peterson Horton and Jessica Carney Smith, *Statistical Record of Black America* (Detroit: Gale Research, 1993), p. 127.

9. Jason DeParle, "Talk of Government Being Out to Get Blacks Falls on More Attentive Ears," *New York Times,* Oct. 29, 1990.

10. Thomas Byrne Edsall with Mary D. Edsall, *Chain Reaction* (New York: W. W. Norton, 1992), p. 239.

11. Dennis Cauchon, "Lock 'Em Up Policy Under Attack," *USA Today,* Sept. 1, 1992.

12. Ron Harris, "Hand of Punishment Falls Heavily on Black Youths," *Los Angeles Times,* Aug. 24, 1993.

13. Ibid.

14. Norval Morris, "Race and Crime," *Judicature* 72 no. 2 (August–September 1988).

## Chapter 9: AIDS and Drugs

1. "HIV/AIDS Program Statistics," Seattle-King County Department of Public Health, www.metrokc.gov/health/apu/stats/statisti.htm, January 5, 1998.

2. Eric Harrison, "AIDS Is No. 1 Killer of Young Americans," *Los Angeles Times,* Dec. 2, 1994.

3. T. Stephen Jones et al., *The Public Health Impact of Needle Exchange Programs in the United States and Abroad* (Berkeley, Calif.: School of Public Health, University of California, 1993), p. 3.

4. Darrell Greene and Barbara Faltz, "Chemical Dependency and Relapse in Gay Men with HIV Infection: Issues and Treatment," in *Counseling Chemically Dependent People with HIV Illness,* ed. Michael Shernoff (New York: Harrington Park Press, 1991), p. 79.

5. James L. Sorenson et al., *Preventing AIDS in Drug Users and Their Sexual Partners* (New York: Guilford Press, 1991), p. 29.
6. "HIV Awareness Figures Up, Study Finds," *Los Angeles Times*, Sept. 29, 1997.
7. "50 HIV Positive Friends," *Narcotics Enforcement and Prevention Digest*, April 13, 1995, p. 5.
8. Jones et al., p. 3.
9. Sorenson et al., p. 33.
10. Michael Powell, "Casualties of the Drug War," *New York Newsday*, July 11, 1993.
11. Sorenson et al., p. 33.
12. Jones et al., p. 3.
13. Stanton Peele, *The Meaning of Addiction* (Lexington, Mass.: Lexington Books, 1985), p. 14.
14. Ibid. p. 15.
15. Andrew Weil and Winifred Rosen, *From Chocolate to Morphine: Everything You Need to Know About Mind-Altering Drugs* (Boston: Houghton Mifflin, 1993), p. 86.
16. Ibid., p. 28.
17. Powell, "Casualties."
18. Jones et al., *Public Health Impact*, p. 4.
19. Ibid., p. 16.
20. Ibid.
21. Peter Reuter, "Hawks Ascendant: The Punitive Trend of American Drug Policy," *Daedalus, Political Pharmacology: Thinking About Drugs*, ed. Stephen R. Graubard, (Summer 1992, Vol. 121, No. 3) p. 42.
22. Edith Springer, "Effective AIDS Prevention with Active Drug Users: The Harm Reduction Model," in *Counseling Chemically Dependent People with HIV Illness*, ed. Michael Shernoff (New York: Harrington Park Press, 1991), p. 147.
23. Ibid., p. 150.
24. Jones et al., *Public Health Impact*, p. 7.
25. Amanda Bennett, "Needle-Swap Programs Spark Life-and-Death Debate," *Wall Street Journal*, July 10, 1996.
26. Ibid., p. 10.
27. Ibid.
28. "Pediatric Group Acknowledges Role of Needle Exchange," *Alcoholism and Drug Abuse Weekly*, Dec. 12, 1994, p. 7.
29. "Where Does the Clinton Administration Stand?" *Drug Policy Letter of the Drug Policy Foundation*, Spring 1994, p. 5.

30. Pamela Warrick, "Some Cities Find Ways to Beat Letter of Law," *Los Angeles Times,* May 23, 1993.

31. Ibid.

32. Tracey Hooker, *Getting to the Point: HIV, Drug Abuse and Syringe Exchange in the United States,* Colorado State Legislative Report, (National Conference of State Legislators, Denver, Colorado), July 1992, Vol. 17, No. 14, p. 6.

33. Ibid., p. 4.

34. Jones et al., *Public Health Impact,* p. 5.

35. Richard C. Paddock, "S.F. Will Provide Drug Users with Clean Needles," *Los Angeles Times,* March 16, 1993.

36. "GAO: Needle Exchanges Show Promise; Surgeon General Could Authorize Fed Funding," *Drug Policy Letter of the Drug Policy Foundation,* June–July 1993, p. 3.

37. Sheryl Stolberg, "Needle Exchange Cuts Risk, Study Finds," *Los Angeles Times,* Jan. 12, 1994.

38. "Studies Say Needle Exchange Programs Don't Abet Drug Use, Help Decrease HIV," *Alcoholism and Drug Abuse Weekly,* Jan. 24, 1994, p. 7.

39. Brenda C. Coleman, "Studies Find Addicts Accept Needle Trades," *San Francisco Examiner,* Jan. 12, 1994.

40. "IOM Report Boosts Needle Exchange as Anti-AIDS Strategy," *Alcoholism and Drug Abuse Weekly,* Aug. 15, 1994, p. 7.

41. Sorenson et al., p. 81.

42. Barry Bearak, "In War on Drugs, Battle Against AIDS Falls Behind," *Los Angeles Times,* Sept. 28, 1992.

## Chapter 10: The Futility of Interdiction

1. "Whatever Happened to the Drug War?" *Frontline* (PBS), February 2, 1993.

2. "ONDCP: Two Thirds of All Drug Money Went to Buy Cocaine in 1995," *Narcotics Enforcement and Prevention Digest,* Nov. 13, 1997, p. 3.

3. "ONDCP Study Confirms Increase in Heroin Availability but Disclaims Alarms of Epidemic," *Narcotics Control Digest,* Aug. 18, 1993, p. 1.

4. "California Study: Drug, Alcohol Use Very High Among Dropouts," *Alcoholism and Drug Abuse Weekly,* Oct. 28, 1992, p. 1.

5. Tim Wells and William Triplett, *Drug Wars: An Oral History from the Trenches* (New York: William Morrow, 1992), p. 52.

6. Jack Anderson and Michael Binstein, "Drug Cartels' Big Planes Are Big Problem," *Washington Post,* Feb. 6, 1995.

7. Jack Anderson and Michael Binstein, "Drugs Coming Out of the Woodwork," *Washington Post*, July 11, 1994.
8. Colin Nickerson, "Harvest of Despair," *Boston Globe*, Nov. 8, 1993.
9. Wells and Triplett, p. 49.
10. "Colombian Poor Lend Stomachs to Drug Trade," *Narcotics Control Digest*, May 26, 1993, p. 9.
11. David Lyons and Christopher Marquis, "Haiti's Military Drug Ties Questioned," *Miami Herald*, June 10, 1994.
12. Carla Anne Robbins, "Mixed Message," *Wall Street Journal*, Aug. 3, 1994.
13. Jim Abrams, "Interdiction Hasn't Stemmed Drug Flow, Congress Is Told," *Boston Globe*, Feb. 26, 1993.
14. "Attorney General Questions Effectiveness of Interdiction and Sentencing Policies," *Narcotics Control Digest*, May 12, 1993, p. 1.
15. Jerome H. Skolnick, "Rethinking the Drug Problem," *Daedalus, Political Pharmacology: Thinking About Drugs*, ed. Stephen R. Graubard, (Summer 1992), Vol. 12, No. 3, p. 145.

## Chapter 11: The World Is a Pusher

1. Tim Golden, "Mexicans Capture Drug Cartel Chief in Prelate's Death," *New York Times*, June 11, 1993.
2. Juanita Darling, "Pope's Envoy Had Meeting with Mexico's Most Wanted," *Los Angeles Times*, Aug. 5, 1994.
3. Juanita Darling, "For Mexico, an Ominous Year of Murder and Revolt," *Los Angeles Times*, May 24, 1994.
4. Steven Wisotsky, *Beyond The War on Drugs*, (Buffalo, N.Y.: Prometheus Books, 1990), p. 12.
5. Douglas Farah, "Colombia's Violent Culture More Durable Than Escobar," *Washington Post*, Dec. 5, 1993.
6. Al Giordano, "Friendly Fire," *The Phoenix*, May 20, 1994.
7. Ibid.
8. Robert D. McFadden, "Head of Medellin Cocaine Cartel Is Killed by Troops in Colombia," *New York Times*, Dec. 3, 1993.
9. Stan Yarbro, "26 Colombian Policemen Die in Siege by Leftist Rebels," *Los Angeles Times*, Nov. 8, 1992.
10. "1997 Andean Coca Estimates," Central Intelligence Agency, Crime and Narcotics Center, Washington, D.C.
11. Corinne Schmidt-Lynch, "On Peru's Hillsides, Coca Farmers Defy U.S. Repression," *San Francisco Examiner-Chronicle*, Sept. 12, 1993.

12. Ibid.
13. Ibid.
14. "1997 Andean Coca Estimates."
15. Thomas Kamm, "Drug War Success Strains Bolivia's Jails," *Wall Street Journal,* April 19, 1993.
16. Marianne W. Zawitz, ed., *Drugs, Crime and the Justice System,* (Washington, D.C.: United States Department of Justice, 1992), p. 37.
17. Vincent T. Bugliosi, *Drugs in America* (New York: Knightsbridge, 1991), p. 43.
18. William Drozdiak, "Balkan War Victor: Heroin," *Washington Post,* Nov. 6, 1993.
19. "U.S. Can't Fight Heroin Imports Without Burma's Cooperation, Brown Says," *Narcotics Control Digest,* June 22, 1994, p. 9.
20. "Americans Switching from Cocaine to Heroin," *Narcotics Control Digest,* April 13, 1994, p. 2.
21. Bob Drogin, "Afghans Going Home — to a Region Littered with Arms, Addicts," *Los Angeles Times,* April 26, 1993.
22. Raymond Bonner, "Joining with the Taliban in a New War on Drugs," *New York Times,* November 30, 1997.
23. Ralph Salerno, "A Policeman's Surveillance Report: Keeping an Eye on the Trail of the Bennett Plan," in *The Great Issues of Drug Policy,* ed. Arnold S. Trebach and Kevin Zeese (Washington, D.C.: Drug Policy Foundation, 1990), p. 63.
24. Byrne, *Drugs and Crime Data,* p. 5.

## Chapter 12: Reducing Societal Damage with a Different Drug Strategy

1. "Pentagon Rethinking Its Drug War Priorities," *Narcotics Control Digest,* Sept. 29, 1993, p. 3; Michael Tackett, "Reno Says Jail Failing in Fight Against Drugs," *San Francisco Examiner-Chronicle,* May 9, 1993.
2. "A Wiser Course: Ending Drug Prohibition," *Record of the Association of Bar of the City of New York* 49, no. 5, June 1994: p. 524.
3. Ronald Hamowy, ed., *Dealing with Drugs* (San Francisco: Pacific Research Institute for Public Policy, 1987), p. 31.
4. "Report Details State/Local Spending on Drug Control," *Drug Policy Letter of the Drug Policy Foundation,* Spring 1994, p. 27.
5. Candice Byrne, *Drugs and Crime Data* (Washington, D.C.: Office of National Drug Control Policy, 1996), p. 5.

6. Arnold S. Trebach, "Thinking Through Models of Drug Legalization," *Drug Policy Letter of the Drug Policy Foundation*, July–August 1994, p. 12.

7. Ibid.

8. Matt Hamblin, "Privatization Lite: The States and Liquor," *Governing*, June 1992, p. 27.

9. Ibid.

10. Michael W. Miller, "Quality Stuff: Firm Is Peddling Cocaine, and Deals Are Legit," *Wall Street Journal*, Oct. 27, 1994.

11. Henry R. Wray, *Confronting the Drug Problem* (Washington, D.C.: General Accounting Office, 1993), p. 27.

12. "100 Leading Advertisers," *Advertising Age*, Sept. 28, 1994, p. 2.

13. 1996 Congressional Justification for the National Institutes of Health, Vol. 7, p. 167.

14. Rudy Abramson, "Tobacco Country," *Los Angeles Times*, Dec. 4, 1994.

15. Tim W. Ferguson, "Calm Down: Risk Is Not All Around," *Wall Street Journal*, Dec. 14, 1993.

16. Ibid.

17. "Lee Brown Speaks Out on Need For Hard-Core Initiative," *Alcoholism & Drug Abuse Weekly*, August 1, 1994, p. 6.

18. Ward S. Condelli, Robert L. Hubbard, "Therapeutic Community Clients Improve with Time in Treatment," *Brown University Digest of Addiction Theory and Application*, October 1994, p. 6.

19. Susan Rosenbaum, "The Star Talks to Dr. Mitchell Rosenthal of Phoenix House," *East Hampton Star*, Oct. 9, 1997, p. II-22.

20. C. Peter Rydell and Susan S. Everingham, *Controlling Cocaine: Supply Versus Demand Programs* (Santa Monica, Calif.: Rand Drug Policy Research Center, 1994), p. 45.

21. Ibid., p. xvi.

22. Sam Vincent Meddis, "Drug Policy Focus: Treatment," *U.S.A. Today*, Oct. 21, 1993.

23. George F. Will, "Our Harmful Drug Policy," *Washington Post*, June 27, 1993.

24. Max Frankel, "Drug War, II," *The New York Times Magazine*, Jan. 29, 1995.

25. "Researchers Find Addicts' Gene Pattern," *Washington Post*, Dec. 29, 1993.

26. Warren E. Leary, "New Enzyme May Curb Cocaine's Addictive Power," *New York Times*, March 26, 1993.

27. Thomas H. Maugh II, "Keys to Body's Pain Control System Found," *Los Angeles Times*, Dec. 18, 1992.

28. Robert Curley, "Addiction Insights," *Alcoholism and Drug Abuse Weekly*, June 27, 1994, p. 5.

29. "Addiction Treatment Drugs Choked Off by Red Tape," *Alcoholism and Drug Abuse Weekly*, July 18, 1994, p. 1.

30. Ralph Salerno, "A Policeman's Surveillance Report: Keeping an Eye on the Trail of the Bennett Plan," in *The Great Issues of Drug Policy*, ed. Arnold S. Trebach and Kevin Zeese (Washington, D.C.: Drug Policy Foundation, 1990), p. 66.

31. Lester Grinspoon, James B. Bakalar, "Costs, Benefits of Drug Legalization — The Debate Continues," *Brown University Digest of Addiction Theory and Application*, August 1994, p. 1.

32. Tim Wells and William Triplett, *Drug Wars* (New York: William Morrow, 1992), p. 18.

33. Marianne W. Zawitz, ed., *Drugs, Crime, and the Justice System* (Washington, D.C.: U.S. Department of Justice, 1992), p. 94.

34. Alonzo L. McDonald, foreword to *Abraham Lincoln: Theologian of American Anguish*, by David Elton Trueblood (New York: HarperCollins, 1973).

35. Richard M. Nixon, *Beyond Peace* (New York: Random House, 1994), p. 239.

# INDEX